THE STORY OF
THE RED CROSS

THE STORY OF
THE RED CROSS

Belinda Peacey

FREDERICK MULLER

First published in Great Britain in 1958 by Frederick Muller
Limited, Fleet Street, London, E.C.4

Copyright © 1958, 1969 Belinda Peacey

Revised 1963
New and revised edition 1969

To
the Boys and Girls of the
British Junior Red Cross

Phototypeset by BAS Printers Limited, Wallop, Hampshire
Printed in Great Britain by Ebenezer Baylis and Son Limited
The Trinity Press, Worcester and London
Bound by Wm. Brendon & Son Ltd., Tiptree
SBN: 584 62034 9

Contents

1	The Man in White	7
2	A Little Book Makes History	17
3	A Red Cross on a White Ground	26
4	The Development of an Ideal	37
5	V.A.D.	48
6	A Delegate of the International Committee	61
7	For Those Behind Barbed Wire	71
8	'Charity in War'	85
9	The Years that Followed	96
10	Korea	107
11	The Red Cross and the Refugees	114
12	The National Societies in Peacetime	134
13	Disasters and Emergencies	153
14	The Junior Sections	170
15	Towards the Unity of Nations	186
	Bibliography	189
	Index	190

Illustrations

Jean Henri Dunant in 1850	10
Solferino	13
The Red Cross, the Red Crescent and the Red Lion and Sun	22-4
The First Genevà Convention, 1864	27
A 'fixed ambulance' in Paris	30
During the Franco-Prussian War	32
A recruitment poster for V.A.D.s	52
A dressing-station at Abbeville, 1917	54
V.A.D. women drivers	55
Refugees of the Spanish Civil War at Hendaye Plage	66
A 'C-International' ship	77
A stretcher-party in action after an air raid	86
Displaced Persons	98
Refugees	101
Sister Ella Jorden with a Korean child	111
Budapest, the Hungarian Uprising of 1956	118
A camp for Hungarian refugees in Austria	119
Medical care for an Algerian refugee	122
Algerian refugee children with Red Cross supplies	123
A floating dispensary in Vietnam	125
Roll-call for Tibetan refugees in Nepal	129
An Outpost Nurse of the Canadian Red Cross tending a lumberman	137
Mountain rescue	143
A Chinese Red Cross member giving first aid to a miner	145
First aid in a harvest field in Hungary	147
An Indian Red Cross rural nurse on a home visit	150
A Red Cross physiotherapist helping a paralysed Moroccan woman	166
Milk for Congolese children	171
A Junior Red Cross member talking to a deaf-blind woman	176
A Red Cross junior at a summer holiday camp	178
A member of the British Junior Red Cross	180

1
The Man in White

On 8th May 1908, an air of excitement spread through the little town of Heiden in the Appenzell Canton of Switzerland overlooking Lake Constance.

The postmaster was probably the first to sense it as the letters, telegrams and parcels poured in from all parts of the world; from emperors and kings, statesmen and politicians as well as ordinary men, women and children. Hour after hour, throughout the day, the bulging mailbags were delivered to the District Hospital for one of the patients, whose eightieth birthday it was.

The occasion was celebrated at the hospital later in the day as quietly and modestly as possible in order not to over-tire the frail old man, who sat at the head of the table wearing a white dressing-gown which some Swedish ladies had made for him. As the glasses were raised to drink his health, he was overcome with emotion and could hardly murmur his thanks.

Presently, baskets of narcissi and irises arrived for him and, from the people of Heiden, a huge red cross embedded in white flowers. This tribute and the inscription on the medal which had been struck to commemorate his birthday reminded all who saw them that Jean Henri Dunant, the man they honoured, was the 'Founder of the Red Cross, 1863: Promoter of the Geneva Convention, 1864'.

But perhaps what pleased the old man most of all was

the telegram he had received from the Federal Council in Berne, his own government, for he was a native of Switzerland. 'It was in the midst of the battle of Solferino that you conceived the idea of organizing societies for the relief of the wounded and sick of the armies in the field,' it read, 'as well as the plan for an agreement of the civilized nations, proclaiming the principles which are the basis of the Convention of Geneva ... This work of international brotherhood and charity in time of war has prospered beyond calculation and now embraces the whole world'.

The words are as true today as they were when they were written. The Red Cross, the 'work of international brotherhood' which owes its origin to Henri Dunant, has indeed 'prospered beyond calculation,' spreading to scores of countries in addition to those which existed in his lifetime.

Henri Dunant had not always lived in Heiden. He had arrived there one July day some twenty years before, sick, impoverished and broken in spirit; reminded, perhaps, by the view of the lake and the mountains around the pleasant little town, of the landscape of his birthplace to which he could never return.

He was born and grew up in Geneva, an enterprising, prosperous city which for centuries had attracted travellers from many countries and given refuge to political and religious reformers, among them John Calvin who, in 1559, had founded the College at which Dunant was educated.

Jean Henri was the eldest of five children of Jean-Jacques Dunant, a wealthy merchant, who came from an old Genevese family and played a leading part in the civic life of Geneva. He was a member of the Council and devoted much of his spare time to charitable works, presiding over an organization for the care and protection of orphans and the welfare of prisoners. From time to time he travelled to Marseilles on business. One day he decided to take his family and go on to Toulon, where he was to inspect the conditions of some of the convicts of Geneva who were serving their sentences there.

The visit to the convict-station was to have a lasting effect upon the six-year-old Henri. When the child saw the convicts exercising in the prison yard and the groups of shackled men breaking stones along the road, he was so distressed that his father had to take him back to the hotel where they were staying. 'When I am big I shall write a book to save them!' the child sobbed. His parents tried to soothe him, but the sights he had seen gave him nightmares from which he suffered for the rest of his life.

Apart from this his childhood was happy. The background of his home and Calvinistic schooling helped to develop in him a keen interest in social work and at the age of twenty-one he founded, with a group of friends, *The Christian Union of Young People*—the Y.M.C.A., which today is known all over the world. He never forgot the convicts he had seen as a child and every Sunday afternoon went to read and talk to the prisoners in the gaol at Geneva.

In June 1853, Mrs Harriet Beecher Stowe visited the city. Her book, *Uncle Tom's Cabin*, published three years before, had caused a sensation throughout the civilized world and deeply impressed Dunant when he read it. He secured an interview with the famous authoress and came away from the meeting fired with the desire to campaign against slavery. His sympathy for convicts, slaves and all who were oppressed and deprived of their liberty was to affect world history in years to come.

Although there was no shortage of money in the Dunant family, Jean-Jacques had decided that his son should have a settled career and apprenticed him to a well-known Genevese banking house with interests abroad. The young Dunant did well at the bank and in August 1853 the directors appointed him accountant to a subsidiary company in Algeria.

The post entailed a certain amount of travelling and Dunant came to know and love the country. A year later he bought a plot of land at Djemila, where he intended to erect flour mills and grow corn, and left the bank to pursue his scheme.

Jean Henri Dunant (seated right) in 1850, at the age of 22

But the land he had bought was useless: a furnace in summer, cold and bleak in winter, without water to irrigate it or turn the millwheels. He was, nevertheless, filled with enthusiasm for the project, and on discovering that there was a waterfall on the adjacent land which belonged to the French government, he went to Constantine to apply for a concession.

While he was awaiting the reply from the governor, he visited Tunisia and wrote a book, a large part of which was devoted to a comparison between slavery there and in the United States.

For the next five years Dunant pursued his Algerian venture; buying more land at great cost, and from time to time returning to Geneva, where he had persuaded a number of his friends to put their money into the Mills of Mons-Djemila, a company he intended to float as soon as he had obtained the concession from the French government.

The year 1859 found him back in Geneva, still without a reply to his application for the land and aware that his enterprise was beginning to show signs of collapse.

Every day the newspapers were filled with accounts of the French armies' achievements in northern Italy, where Napoleon III was engaged in a war to free the Italians from Austrian rule. As Dunant read of the campaign, a bold thought entered his head: he would obtain an interview with Napoleon, to whom he wished to dedicate his forthcoming book on the Roman Empire, and secure from him the concession he so urgently needed.

Armed with a copy of the book beautifully printed and bound, a well-filled purse and a large amount of luggage, he hired a carriage at the beginning of June and left for

Italy. Changing from one conveyance to another, he rattled over roads damaged by fighting, forded rivers where bridges had been blown up, driving all through the night in his haste to reach the Emperor. At Brescia, he employed as a driver an army deserter who knew where Napoleon was to be found. The signs of fighting were everywhere as they drew nearer to the battle zone; and towards nightfall a few days later Dunant was driven into the little town of Solferino, overlooking a great plain lying to the south of Lake Garda.

But he did not see the Emperor. He had arrived on the scene of hideous devastation which followed one of the fiercest battles of the nineteenth century. At Solferino, on Friday 24th June, over three hundred thousand men had been engaged in the fighting, which had started at three o'clock that morning and raged furiously for fifteen hours in the scorching heat of mid-summer, until a violent thunderstorm had brought the battle to an end. The Austrians, withdrawing their forces, retreated across the Mincio, pursued by the French and Piedmontese.

It had been a costly battle in men and lives for both victors and the vanquished; the casualties numbering about forty thousand. Although the armies had collected as many of them as they could carry in military wagons and requisitioned carts, the darkness and heavy rain had hampered their efforts and in the haste of their departure they had abandoned the larger part of their dead and wounded out in the open where they lay. All through the night soldiers went searching for their comrades on the battlefield.

The next day the sun rose over a countryside strewn with dead and dying men. The work of collecting and

...ferino, the village which gave the battle its name, with the ancient watch-tower 'the Spy of Italy', on the summit of a hill

helping them began immediately, continuing throughout the next three days.

The casualties were loaded on to stretchers, mule-packs and wagons and taken to the nearest town or village, in which every available building was turned into an improvised hospital. By far the largest number was brought into the small village of Castiglione, where fresh convoys arrived every quarter of an hour. Soon the hospital, five churches, a monastery, police and military barracks and private houses were filled with wounded men. As more arrived, straw was spread out in the streets for them to lie on and, here and there, rough wooden shelters were put up to shade them from the sun.

The overcrowding was indescribable. The surgeons worked tirelessly, but there were not nearly enough of them, and for lack of hands to carry out the simplest tasks men were dying in hundreds. Heat, flies and thirst added to their misery.

Dunant had gone down to the plain to help, and as he viewed that appalling spectacle of human suffering he was filled with horror and pity. But fortunately for the future history of mankind, his emotions had a practical side and he immediately realized the first essential. A volunteer service must be organized to help the hard-pressed surgeons, make dressings, take food and water to the sick and dying. By the Sunday morning he had succeeded in forming a band of helpers among the women of Castiglione and several tourists who were in the town.

Later he wrote, 'The women entered the churches and went from one man to another with jars and canteens full of water to quench their thirst ... The gentleness and kindness and compassion of these improvised nurses and their attentive care helped to revive a little courage among the patients.'

He enrolled the children as water-carriers.

'I sought to organize as best I could relief in the quarters where it seemed to be most lacking,' he wrote, 'and I adopted in particular one of the Castiglione churches called, I think, the Chiesa Maggiore.'

Nearly five hundred soldiers had been crowded into this church and forgotten; a hundred more lay on straw outside. Dunant found water for the thirsting, changed dressings, laid fresh lint on wounds, gave out tobacco (for many of the men believed that the smoke acted as a disinfectant). Night and day he toiled, begrudging every hour of sleep which took him from his work.

As he came and went in his white tropical clothes the rows of wounded men followed him with their gaze. They gave him the name of 'the Man in White' and it was for him they called out in their moments of worst suffering.

Many nationalities were to be found among them—French, Arab, German, Slav, Croat, Hungarian, Italian. 'But the women of Castiglione,' he wrote, 'on observing that I made no distinction of nationality, followed my example and showed the same samaritan care to every one of these men of such divers origins, men who by the same token were foreigners to them ... As they went about their tasks they murmered, "*Tutti fratelli*—all are brothers".'

Dunant realized that the soldiers, in addition to their physical sufferings, were tortured by homesickness and anxiety for their families. 'Oh sir, if you could write to my father to comfort my mother!' cried a young corporal, an only son, who had joined the army as a volunteer and now lay dying. His name, like that of many another, appeared in the lists of missing and the only news his parents received of him was in the letter Dunant wrote to them. 'A Neuchatel merchant,' he recorded, 'devoted himself for two whole days to dressing wounds and writing farewell letters to their families for dying men.'

Three days after Dunant had organized the work he called for his carriage and drove to the French military headquarters at Borghetto, where he pleaded that the Austrian doctors who had been captured should be brought to the help of their wounded. At his request they were released and took over some of the work of the exhausted surgeons.

On his way back to Castiglione he bought comforts for the wounded: camomile, mallow, oranges, lemons, sugar, shirts, tobacco and various dainties unprocurable locally.

He spent nearly five weeks in the village. In time the casualties were removed to hospitals in the larger towns and cities where they would receive better attention; the overcrowding lessened and, after satisfying himself that everything was in hand for their care, Dunant returned home.

His experiences were to alter the entire course of his life. 'I have seen a human being die in unimaginable agonies every fifteen minutes,' he wrote from Solferino to a friend. Thousands of men had survived the battle to die afterwards through lack of proper care and attention. He and his band of helpers had touched only the bare fringe of the mass of suffering; what they had done had been better than nothing; but it had not been enough.

Something more was needed.

2

A Little Book Makes History

Dunant arrived back at Geneva worn out in mind and body by his experiences. He could think and talk of nothing but the horrifying results of the battle of Solferino. He took a holiday in the mountains, visited Paris, but nothing would rid his thoughts of the agony and death he had seen. Finally he decided to write a book, drawing public attention to the inadequacy of the care given to the wounded and the necessity of remedying it; and shutting himself away from his friends, he set to work.

He called the book *A Memory of Solferino*. Beginning with a factual account of the battle, he went on to describe the ghastly plight of its victims, sparing his readers none of the harrowing details. He told of the band of helpers he had organized, their devoted work and the compassion they had shown to friend and enemy without distinction. Towards the end of the book he wrote,

> 'But why have I recounted all these scenes of pain and distress and perhaps aroused painful emotions in my readers?'

and answered the question by asking another,

> 'Would it not be possible in time of peace and quiet, to form relief societies for the purpose of having care given to the wounded in wartime by zealous, devoted and

thoroughly qualified volunteers? ... Societies of this kind, once formed and their permanent existence assured ... would be always organized and ready for the possibility of war. They would not only have to secure the goodwill of the authorities of the countries in which they had been formed, but also, in case of war, to solicit from the rulers of the belligerent states authorization and facilities enabling them to do effective work.'

A Memory of Solferino is a modest little book, but written with such burning sincerity that no one who reads it can help being moved by it. Dunant published it at his own expense in November 1862.

The book caused an immediate sensation. Very soon everyone in Europe was reading and talking about it and messages by the hundred poured in to the author. Among its admirers was Charles Dickens, who published several extracts from it in his magazine *All the Year Round*, and Gustave Moynier, a prominent lawyer in Geneva and president of the city's Society for Public Welfare, who was so impressed by Dunant's ideas that he came in person to say, 'Monsieur Dunant, you have had a very fine inspiration!'

Through Moynier a special Committee of Five, composed of himself, Dunant and three others, was set up to discuss the formation of relief societies such as were advocated in the book.

That Committee was the predecessor of the International Committee of the Red Cross, the impartial, independent body which exists in Geneva today. It is recruited from Swiss citizens and its membership may not exceed twenty-five.

The word 'international' in the Committee's title refers not to its membership but its work, which is carried on almost entirely outside its own country and is of particular importance in time of war or armed conflict, when the Committee's special function is to act as a neutral intermediary and provide a channel through which relief can be sent to the victims of war in countries at war.

The Committee's exclusively Swiss membership is the chief guarantee of its neutrality; for not only has Switzerland been neutral for centuries, but in the interests of Europe the Great Powers in 1815 granted her perpetual neutrality.

The Red Cross, by its strict observance of this principle, has earned the confidence and respect of governments and statesmen, who know that in the unique work it is called upon to do in war it can be trusted never to serve the interests of one side to the detriment of the other.

The idea of granting neutral status to the relief societies was in Dunant's mind from the outset; and when Moynier proposed that the practical details for establishing them should be discussed at an international meeting called by the Committee of Five in Geneva, Dunant insisted that the question of an international treaty for the protection of the societies should be raised at the same time. But Moynier considered this was making excessive demands; their foundation must first be secured.

He and Dunant were too diverse in character to work together for long: the one, a visionary, impulsive and enthusiastic, lacked the critical faculty and methodical, well-trained mind of the other, who was destined to become the first president of the International Committee and to hold the office for over forty years. As events were later to prove, the Red Cross movement owed an equal debt to the contribution of both men.

Shortly after the meeting of the Committee of Five, Dunant went to Paris and thence to Berlin, where he attended a Statistical Congress at which a number of influential people were present. At banquets, receptions and other social functions, he urged everyone he met to support the forthcoming meeting in Geneva and, in particular, his proposal for an international agreement.

'What does this man Dunant want? And whatever does he think the King has to do with his notions of welfare?' the Prussian Minister for War asked Doctor Basting, a Dutch surgeon-major.

'He is anxious to establish the neutral status on the battlefield of the wounded and those who go to their help,' replied Doctor Basting, who was much in sympathy with Dunant's idea.

'Ah, that is a different thing! I shall explain it to the King,' said the Minister.

From Berlin, Dunant went to Dresden, Munich and Vienna (each of which was a capital city in those days) where he was received by royalty and granted interviews by ministers of State. Encouraged by his success, he had printed a circular stressing the need for the relief societies to be officially recognized and granted neutral status, and sent a copy to everyone who had agreed to attend the Geneva meeting.

On his return two days before it opened, he reported his triumphs to the Committee of Five.

'And what did you think of my circular?' he asked eagerly.

'We think you are asking the impossible,' Moynier

replied in icy tones. He was filled with apprehension lest Dunant had compromised the success of the meeting and was convinced that the revolutionary ideas expressed in the circular would never be carried by the delegates.

Despite Moynier's fears the Geneva meeting, which opened on 26th October, was a great success and as a result of Dunant's efforts was attended by representatives from fourteen countries. Moynier, who presided, felt they had achieved their purpose once general agreement had been reached on the plans to set up in every country national committees, or societies, for the care of wounded on the battlefield. The foundation of the movement, later to be known as the Red Cross, had been laid.

Dunant, who had been appointed secretary and took the notes at the meeting, realized that the first part of his great idea put forward in *A Memory of Solferino* was firmly on the way to becoming a reality.

There matters would have rested, had Moynier had his way. But now Doctor Basting leapt to his feet and insisted that Dunant's circular should be discussed. Moynier was obliged to continue.

The representatives fully approved the recommendations; but as they were not empowered with the authority to speak for their governments, proposed that a diplomatic conference should be held to decide these matters.

The meeting ended, the representatives returned to their countries. The immediate task before them was the setting up of national committees or relief societies. The first society was formed within weeks of the Geneva meeting, in the State of Würtemberg, which later merged with Germany. It is the Belgian Red Cross which holds pride of place as the oldest of the national societies, and celebrated its centenary in February 1964.

The Red Cross trucks in the Second World War
(see page 94)

Ten countries in 1864 announced the formation of societies, one of which, the French society, Dunant helped to found; and in the next twenty years societies were established in the Middle East and Latin American countries. In the beginning they went by a variety of titles—the Geneva meeting not having settled on a precise name for them—and it was the Dutch society, established in 1867, which first included the words 'Red Cross' in its title. The designation was later adopted by a large number of the societies.

But the emblem raised a problem in some countries,

for although the red cross is not a religious symbol and never figured as such among the Christian countries which adopted it, the device proved unacceptable to Turkey, the first non-Christian country to establish a relief society. Memories of the age-long struggle between the Crescent and the Cross still lingered in 1876 when Turkey dissolved its 'Aid Society to the Wounded', formed eight years before, and re-established it with the name and emblem of the Red Crescent, which several other Moslem countries subsequently adopted. Russia (whose first national society was established in 1867) with its large Moslem population uses both the crescent and

A Tunisian Red Crescent truck with supplies for Algerian refugees (see page 123)

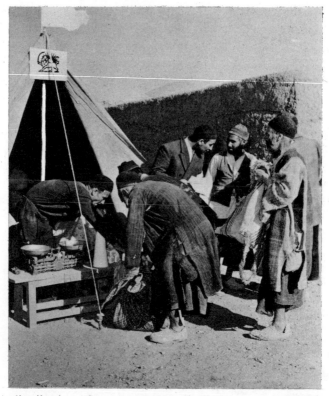

A distribution of emergency supplies by the Persian Red Lion and Sun Society

the cross, and since 1925 the organization has been known as the Alliance of Red Cross and Red Crescent Societies of the U.S.S.R.

In 1922 the Persians (Moslems of a different rite from the Turks) took the Red Lion and Sun.

The International Red Cross conference of 1949, realizing the confusion that would arise if any more signs were added to those which already existed, refused to agree to Israel's adoption of the Red Shield of David; the Magen Adom David is not, therefore, part of the Red Cross movement although it does very similar work.

3
A Red Cross on a White Ground

The eyes of Europe had been turned towards the little meeting at Geneva; so when the Committee of Five approached the Swiss Federal Council with the request for a diplomatic conference to be held there instead of in Berne, the Council readily gave its consent and officially invited to the conference government representatives with authority to sign the international agreement which Dunant had striven so hard to achieve.

The conference was held in the Town Hall and to it sixteen countries sent delegates; several of them the same men who had attended the Geneva meeting ten months before. Within a fortnight they had drawn up a treaty, which was signed on 22nd August 1864 and bears the name *The Convention of Geneva*.

It was the first international agreement of its kind and one of the greatest treaties in the history of the civilized world. Countless millions of fighting men owe their lives to the rights and conditions secured for them under the terms of the Geneva Convention and the later conventions for which it paved the way. It recognized that a soldier once he is wounded ceases to be an enemy and becomes a suffering, defenceless human being, deserving of sympathy and tender care. It lays down that the ambulance that carries him, the hospital to which he is taken, and the doctors, nurses and all personnel who are entrusted with his care, shall be protected.

The adoption of a distinctive emblem for the people and establishments placed under this special protection was an important part of this international agreement. In honour of Switzerland this was to be a red cross on a white ground, obtained by reversing the colours of the Swiss flag. Later the red crescent and the red lion and sun on a white ground became the recognized symbols of protection for the countries which had adopted them instead of the red cross.

A red cross on a white armlet was worn on a battle-field some months before its use was officially recognized by the diplomatic conference in Geneva. In the spring of

The First Geneva Convention, 1864, 'for the Amelioration of the Condition of the Wounded in Armies in the Field', established the principle of impartial aid for the sick and wounded, irrespective of whether they are friends or enemies, and the neutrality of all personnel and establishments concerned in their care

1864 when the war of the Duchies broke out between Prussia and Denmark, the Committee of Five appointed one of its members, Doctor Louis Appia, to carry out a mission with the Prussian army. He later reported that his Red Cross armlet had given him entry everywhere.

Meanwhile, the man who had given the first impulse to the national committees and the international treaty— the 'Founder of the Red Cross' and 'Promoter of the Geneva Convention' as his birthday medal was to proclaim him nearly fifty years afterwards—was fading from the public scene. He was not even present in the conference chamber when the Geneva Convention was signed.

In his efforts to establish the Red Cross, Dunant had neglected his business and his affairs were now in a bad way. The year after the Convention was signed Napoleon III paid a State visit to Algeria; Dunant arranged to be there at the same time and obtained from the Emperor the promise of his patronage of the French Red Cross. While in Algeria, he had also to face the sorry sight of his Mons-Djemila Company. Drought had killed his cattle and immobilized his mills and his stewards had robbed him during his long absences. Two years later he was declared bankrupt, a grave social stigma for a Genevan. Deprived of his citizenship, he resigned from the International Committee and left his native city never to return.

He went now to live in Paris, where he found cheap lodgings in the poor quarter and managed to keep his head above water by occasional translation, secretarial and journalistic work. Cold, hunger and his dejected state brought on the first bouts of a nervous complaint from which he suffered acutely in later years.

Soon after he came to Paris the first International Conference of the Red Cross Societies was held in the city. The extension of the terms of the Geneva Convention to the casualties of naval warfare and the protection of hospital ships was discussed and Dunant, who had already suggested these measures, also prepared a memorandum on prisoners of war to lay before the meeting; but nothing came of it.

He continued to live in Paris and was there in 1870 when the Franco-Prussian war was declared.

It was this war which brought the British Red Cross Society into action for the first time.

In its early days the Red Cross had been described as 'a good thought until it should become a good work'; but although Britain had sent representatives to the meeting and the diplomatic conference at Geneva, the British Red Cross remained 'a good thought' until 1870.

In *A Memory of Solferino* Dunant had expressed his admiration of Florence Nightingale's work in the Crimea, but the vast reforms of the army medical services which she had carried out after her return were, perhaps, the reason why the need for such an organization as the Red Cross was less keenly felt in the United Kingdom than in some countries.

On 22nd July, Colonel Loyd Lindsay, V.C., a Crimean veteran, wrote a letter to *The Times* suggesting that a committee should be formed and funds raised to send help to the wounded of both sides in the Franco-Prussian war, and himself opened the appeal with a contribution of £1,000. The public's response was immediate: France had been Britain's ally in the Crimean War and Queen Victoria had relations on the Prussian side, so British sympathy was divided. Within a week of the publication of the letter a society was formed, and three weeks later surgeons, nurses and agents, fully equipped for their task, crossed the Channel.

The German Red Cross was extremely well organized, with a Central Committee in Berlin and a network of over two thousand committees spread over Germany, from which relief could flow right through to the field of battle. As the troops moved farther away from their own territory and it became more difficult to reach the wounded, railway trains, specially adapted as travelling hospitals and capable of carrying as many as nine hundred men on one journey, were devised. These ambulance trains were the first of their kind in Europe. At every halting place of importance along the line hospitals were set up, to which were removed the sick and wounded men who

A 'fixed ambulance' at the Théâtre Français in Paris

could be taken no further without risk to their condition.

For the French Red Cross the organization of medical aid became far more difficult with the rapid succession of military defeats inflicted upon the French armies. The Central Committee in Paris established at the railway stations fixed ambulances to receive the wounded and information bureaux for soldiers' families. Before long communication with Paris was cut off and the provincial committees took the initiative in setting up hospitals and forming ambulances which left for the various battle-fronts.

A number of Americans who were living in Paris when the war broke out joined forces with the first surgeons and nurses sent from England and made up the Anglo-American Ambulance. The units were in the thick of the fighting throughout the war. Constantly under fire, the surgeons and their helpers worked devotedly under difficult conditions, often performing serious operations by candlelight under a hail of gunfire and bullets. Arriving at Sedan on the eve of the German breakthrough, they dealt with the heavy casualties there and after the fall of Metz. When supplies of food were cut off they went without so that their patients should have what there was. As far north as the Belgian frontier the British surgeons were at work in the emergency hospitals; some went to Orleans, others established a hospital at Épernay. All through the war the London Committee kept its workers with the German and French sides supplied with all their needs. On one occasion the London Committee received a telegram from a German hospital at Pont-à-Mousson on the Moselle, asking for two hundred and fifty iron bedsteads. Forty-eight hours later they had arrived at their destination from the other side of the Channel.

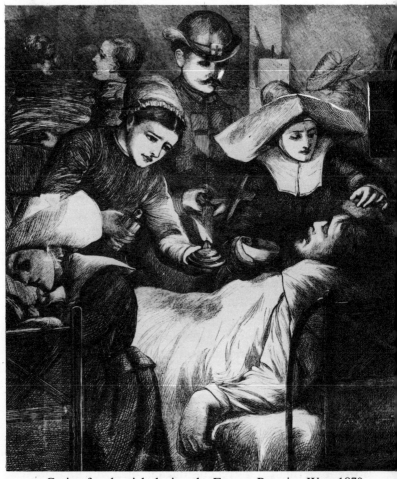

Caring for the sick during the Franco-Prussian War, 1870

One of the British society's last acts in this war was to give a donation of £20,000 each to the German and French societies. Colonel Loyd Lindsay came over to deliver the money in person. He was received at Versailles by the King of Prussia, who 'was a little huffy at the proposed division of the money, remarking, "You are certainly very impartial, indeed".'

Handing over the French share presented numerous difficulties. Colonel Loyd Lindsay was warned that he crossed the army lines at his own risk, but accomplished his mission safely thanks to the protection of the Geneva Convention and his Red Cross arm-band, which was saluted by soldiers and peasants everywhere.

Near the porcelain factory at Sèvres, he was ordered to leave his carriage. Then, preceded by a trumpeter on horseback with a white flag fastened to his sword, a Hussar officer also on horseback, and his servant carrying a little bag and a Red Cross flag, the party marched in solemn silence to the barricade at the end of the long deserted street where they were ordered to halt. The trumpeter, sounding a blast and waving his white flag, advanced. 'I felt a little uneasy for the poor man's safety,' Colonel Loyd Lindsay said afterwards, 'because Count Bismark had told me that the objection to a *parlementaire* was that a trumpeter was generally used up on each occasion.' He recognized the French barricade from the little white flag fluttering above it and the French heads which popped up to take a cautious look at them as they drew nearer.

The bridge over the Seine was damaged and the party had to cross in a rowing boat. An hour later they were safely over and arrived at the village of Boulogne-sur-Seine, where a carriage awaited Colonel Loyd Lindsay to convey him to the French Red Cross to whom he handed over the British gift.

Shortly before the outbreak of the war, Clara Barton, who in the American Civil War had undertaken similar work to that of the Red Cross, was staying in Geneva. While she was there she paid a visit to Moynier, who asked her to use her influence with the American government and persuade them to ratify the Geneva Convention. She eventually succeeded in doing this in 1882, a year after she had formed the American Red Cross.

She was in Berne when the Franco–Prussian war was declared and immediately put off her return to the United States to go to Karlsruhe to help the German Red Cross. Towards the end of September when Strasbourg fell, she left for the city and there organized relief for the civilians who had been left homeless after the bombardment and were at the point of starvation. In giving aid to the civilian victims she began what has subsequently become a characteristic activity of the American Red Cross.

At Basle, the International Committee had organized a depot for the collection and distribution of relief for the wounded. Miss Barton found 'a larger supply than I had ever seen at any one time. The trains were loaded with boxes and barrels pouring in from Austria and northern Italy,' she wrote to a friend, '... and every box, package or barrel marked with a broad, bright scarlet cross, which rendered it safe from molestation'.

The red cross on a white ground and what it represented had fired everyone's imagination. Its appeal found an echo not only in the heart of Europe but as far away as Java, the most distant of the Dutch colonies. Gifts of all kinds and money poured in for the men wounded in battle. Everyone—high and low, rich and poor—wished to contribute his bit towards the relief of suffering. Among the donations from Sweden were Fl.224 (about £14 in those days) from two companies of little ship boys.

Russia and Austria sent money and gifts; Spain and Portugal brought out wines from their cellars. Hospitals and convalescent homes were opened in Milan and on Lake Maggiore where, a writer of the time says, 'officers whose broken health required a milder climate were located under a genial sky and obtained a more rapid and complete cure'.

Another national society which, like the British, made its first contribution to the work of mercy at this time was that of the small Duchy of Luxembourg. The society undertook the management and forwarding of the Red Cross stores which arrived at the frontier from Holland and Belgium, and as soon as war broke out thirty-three doctors and assistants hastened to offer their services. As famine spread in and around Sedan after the French surrender, the people of Luxembourg touchingly displayed their charity, taking it in turn to provide bread for the starving soldiers.

Switzerland, which had formed a Red Cross society in 1866, also showed great charity towards her suffering neighbour. When a French army of eighty-five thousand, of whom over five thousand were sick and wounded, arrived in Switzerland destitute and asking for help, the inhabitants of this small State did not hesitate to provide them with everything that they needed. One of the English doctors who accompanied the French troops as they were marched into Switzerland to be interned, wrote of the piteous condition they were in: 'Hundreds of poor fellows, their uniforms torn to rags, limped along; the feet and hands of nearly all were frost-bitten causing the greatest pain. For weeks none had washed, changed his clothes or removed his boots. Nothing but hurried march and counter-march.'

The International Committee of the Red Cross arranged for the repatriation of French invalided soldiers in Germany and obtained the release of two thousand five hundred men, taking care of them on the journey back to their native land.

But when the Committee was asked to intervene in favour of prisoners of war and the French soldiers who were interned in Switzerland, it refused. 'The Red Cross is the emblem of the relief service,' Moynier asserted, and ought not to be used to help men who were in good health.

He lacked the vision of Henri Dunant, who saw prisoners of war as the victims of war and had tried repeatedly to secure rights and a status for them.

Despite his efforts, forty-three years were to elapse before the basic principle that 'Prisoners of war must be humanely treated' was embodied in a humanitarian convention.

4

The Development of an Ideal

Dunant had had less to do with the French Red Cross since his financial troubles and throughout the Franco-Prussian war he remained in Paris following a line of his own. 'I have now a part to play of the greatest importance,' he wrote to his brother.

He occupied himself almost entirely with various welfare schemes for the troops, arranging concerts and lectures for them and founding a society to provide each man with a woollen blanket and case of field dressings, which he distributed himself. He also organized for the benefit of the wounded parties and shows, at which famous French actors and comedians gave their services under the sign of the Red Cross.

After the battle of Sedan on 1st September, Napoleon III and his entire army surrendered to the King of Prussia. Napoleon left for England where he ended his days in exile and a new government was formed in Paris.

While the fighting continued in other parts of France, the King of Prussia's armies arrived before the capital. They made no attempt to take it by siege, hoping to break its resistance by blockade. As they anticipated, food began to be scarce. In the shops the supplies of horse-flesh and donkey meat soon gave place to dogs, cats and even rats, and by the end of December, when, amazed and exasperated by the Parisians' resistance, the Prussians decided to bombard the city, the lack of food was becoming critical. Without warning, the siege guns opened fire; but full of courage and patriotism, the people continued to hold out.

The Central Committee of the French Red Cross worked on throughout the shelling of the city, caring for hundreds of wounded at the Barrack Hospital in the Cours-la-Reine, to which civilian casualties needing attention were also brought in from the streets.

On 28th January, when supplies of food in Paris were practically exhausted, an armistice was signed. The Prussians immediately sent large quantities of food into the starving city; provisions also arrived from the London Committee of the British Red Cross.

The short occupation of Paris ended with a victory march of thirty thousand Prussian troops through the streets on 3rd March. Every door and window was barred and the citizens observed a day of mourning. Left to themselves, they vented their rage on those who had brought humiliation upon them by surrendering to the enemy.

The Commune, the name given to the period of lawlessness and revolt which now broke out, when a political faction attemped to replace the National Assembly, continued for the two following months. The great majority of the Parisians took no part in the activities of the Communards, many of whom were foreigners living in Paris at this time. The Commune was essentially international in its character.

Dunant lost no time in making his way to the Communard authorities to plead with them to observe the terms of the Geneva Convention in the event of a civil war. He was assured that there would be no war and that the Red Cross would be allowed to continue its work unhindered. Both these assurances proved to be empty. Barely a month later when the Barrack Hospital was filled with wounded, over a hundred of whom were Communards, a Communard doctor arrived with orders to take it over. The Red Cross protested and refused to abandon the building or haul down their flag. For a time the hospital was under the command of both doctors, working side by side bitterly resenting each other's presence. In time the Communard doctor's authority faded and the hospital returned to normal once more.

About this time the French Red Cross asked Dunant to act as a neutral intermediary, and intercede with the Prussians at Versailles to spare the lives of two partisans who had attempted to defend their homes against the invaders. The men were wounded, and when they recovered were to be shot. Dunant at once accepted the task, and although arrested by a sentry on his way to the Prussian headquarters, he succeeded in obtaining not only his own release but also that of the condemned men.

After the armistice a large number of the more prosperous citizens had left Paris; and as the fighting in the streets grew more violent Dunant devised a plan to help others to get away. During the siege all railway stations had been closed with the exception of the Gare du Nord, from which trains left for Saint-Denis, the one gate out of Paris kept open by the Prussians. To leave by this exit a foreign passport and a permit signed by a Communard officer had to be produced. Geneva had deprived Dunant of his citizenship, but he still had his Swiss passport, and without pausing to consider the consequences had he been caught, he lent it time and again to some poor fugitive enabling him to pass through the barrier and board the train to safety.

Those who examined the travellers' papers seemed never to detect the repeated journeys the same document was making. For hours afterwards Dunant would linger near the station, buying an occasional drink or newspaper, avoiding the glances of the people around him while he waited for the passport to be brought back to him by a railway superintendent, who was in the conspiracy, from a safe halt up the line.

Shortly afterwards he used the passport himself to leave from the Gare du Nord; the purpose of his journey was to discuss with the Prussians at Versailles a plan for evacuating the women and children from Paris. By now French guns were trained against the city; the streets were blocked by barricades, obstinately defended and captured only after fierce fighting. Both sides were guilty of taking hostages and massacring innocent victims, many of whom were women and children. It had even been found necessary to close the Barrack Hospital, and the French Red Cross had difficulty in finding a place elsewhere to which the patients could be removed. But the Prussian troops watched the bombardment of the twice-besieged city and would not interfere.

On the evening of 24th May an ancient prophecy that Paris would be burnt by its citizens was fulfilled. The Seine gleamed and flickered with the reflections of the Hotel de Ville, the Tuileries and other famous buildings which had been set alight. The Archbishop of Paris and several other hostages were shot by the Communards, in revenge for the treatment of some of their men in the hands of the Versailles troops.

Dunant was powerless. His efforts to bring about an armistice between the belligerents had failed; his pleas to spare the hostages were ignored. The Red Cross no longer had the power to restrain the savagery which seized the desperate mob. Anyone was likely to be denounced as a spy and led before a firing squad, more especially a foreigner. His only hope of survival, like that of many others, was to go into hiding.

With the fall of the last barricade to the Versailles troops on 28th May, the fighting came to an end. A French historian has written, 'It is reckoned that seventeen thousand men perished in this horrible mêlée ... Paris lost altogether eighty thousand citizens'.

Dunant had lived through it all. To his memory of Solferino he now added memories of the grim sufferings during the seige of Paris and the reprisals which followed the Commune, when thousands of people were put to death or sent to the penal colonies.

The sight of the captives being rounded up and led through the streets to be deported did not alone make Dunant decide to do something for them. Sympathy for men deprived of their liberty had its roots in his childhood's experience at Toulon; the arbitrary treatment to which prisoners of war were subjected had occupied his thoughts constantly since he came to live in Paris. He had brought out a pamphlet in which he put forward practical suggestions for their physical and moral care and made a plea for safeguards to protect them.

In those days prisoners of war were entirely at the mercy of their captors. Belligerents undertook to allow them a minimum of food and shelter to keep them alive until settlement was made at the end of hostilities, but little else was done for them. Dunant's pamphlet demanded more humane treatment for them. He urged that steps should be taken to provide them during their captivity with what was necessary for their well-being; that they should be given facilities to correspond with their families and friends and their journeys to camp or for repatriation should be made as comfortable as possible for them; that those who died should have decent burial and their relatives be informed of the time and place of death. Finally, he put forward the startling suggestion that good feeling should be encouraged between a prisoner and his captors.

On learning that his ideas were sympathetically received in England, he resolved to go to London where, he felt sure, he would be able to convince people of the need for an international treaty for the protection of prisoners of war. He would arouse public opinion, use his powers of persuasion as he had used them to gain support for the Geneva meeting. But, he reflected, he was now alone; there was no Society for Public Welfare to give him its support. He was discredited and a bankrupt —facts that weighed heavily on his conscience—short of funds and a sick man. Even so, borrowing some money from his brother Pierre, he booked a room at the St James's Hotel in Piccadilly and arrived there in August 1872.

It was stiflingly hot in London. The privations he had endured throughout the war in Paris were beginning to tell on him, and on a tour of St Thomas's Hospital he collapsed and had to be escorted back to his hotel. He had developed eczema in his right hand and at times it was so painful he could scarcely write.

But the prisoners' cause, for which he felt as fervently as he had that of the wounded of Solferino, spurred him on. He addressed a gathering at the Royal Society of Arts in the Adelphi and meetings in Plymouth and Brighton. He was well reported in *The Times*, but lacked the funds to go and lecture as he was asked to in Liverpool and Manchester. Florence Nightingale expressed interest in his ideas and invited him to spend a few days at Claydon, her Buckinghamshire home, but he was too unwell and poverty-stricken to accept her invitation.

About this time he made the acquaintance of a Mrs Coombes, who kept a girls' boarding-school called Broadlands, in Flodden Road, Camberwell. She gave him a room when his hand became too painful to use and nursed him back to health.

He left England a year or two later with none of his aims achieved; and for the next twelve years wandered from place to place, living in poverty and obscurity mainly in Stuttgart, occasionally in England and sometimes Heiden. He disappeared from public life and it was widely supposed, even in Geneva, that he must be dead. In 1887 he returned to Heiden where he spent the rest of his days.

He was fifty-nine when he came to Heiden; but with his flowing white beard and shabby clothes he looked an old man. The children certainly thought so as they watched him make his way down the street and turn in at the Paradise Inn.

As soon as he had settled into his room at the inn he asked the proprietress to find him a doctor. Doctor Altherr came at once and from then on looked after his health, taking a great interest in him and often inviting him to his house.

In time all the people of Heiden came to know Dunant. The children liked the old man who talked to them in his 'funny' German; their parents held him in great esteem. With normal care and attention his health improved; but as his hand still needed treatment Doctor Altherr arranged for him to have a room in the District Hospital.

Eight years later Georg Baumberger, a young journalist from St Gall, was spending a holiday in Heiden and heard of the old man who was living there. When he discovered who he was, he realized he had a first class story for his paper and asked for an interview with Dunant.

A day or two later, Baumberger was shown into Room 12 at the District Hospital, where seated before him was an elderly man with a patriarchial beard, wearing a dark dressing-gown and smoking-cap. 'It is I who founded the Red Cross,' the man said. Henri Dunant, whose book *A Memory of Solferino* had shaken Europe thirty-three years before, was still alive.

Baumberger's story was published and brought fame again to Dunant. It brought letters from old friends who had lost touch with him and tributes and messages from famous people, Red Cross and other societies. The news that he was alive also brought gifts of money from several of his friends who were deeply touched to learn of his poverty, and from the Dowager Empress of Russia a pension, which kept him in reasonable comfort for the rest of his days.

Dunant continued to live in the room at the District Hospital under Doctor Altherr's care, but he was now back in public life. His opinion was sought on many matters, distinguished people visited him; he received honours, his birthdays were formally celebrated. The recognitions brought some measure of happiness and peace to his troubled conscience.

A few years later he read with satisfaction that The Hague Convention of July 1899 extended the provisions of the Geneva Convention to the victims of war at sea. Under its terms hospital ships of the belligerents were to be painted green, with a white stripe; those of the relief societies, white with a red stripe. Both were to fly the Red Cross flag and their crews could not be taken captive.

The measures were introduced three months before the British Red Cross had recourse to them in fitting out a hospital ship which, with two hospital trains, was among its chief contributions to the medical services in the South African War. The hospital ship, *The Princess of Wales*, brought seven hundred and twenty-eight wounded men safely home to England during the war; and so well was she equipped that of all those who were treated on board only one man died.

The idea of a hospital train came from Princess Christian, and the first of the two trains was named after her. It was built in Birmingham and, after being inspected by her, was taken to pieces and shipped out to South Africa to be reassembled. The train saved thousands of lives and, as the first to be allowed into Ladysmith after the siege had been lifted, its entry was a dramatic and memorable event. The bridge over the Tugela River had been blown up by the Boers and on the farther bank *The Princess Christian* waited, while the last rivets were hastily driven into a trestle bridge to bring her over.

The second hospital train was commandeered at East London railway station by two Red Cross officers, who had for some time been endeavouring without success to obtain one through the correct channels. As this troop train captured from the Boers drew into the station, the officers promptly ordered it off to the railway-yard to be painted white. Hardly was the work completed than an urgent call came through to say the train was needed at once for military purposes up country. 'Well,' replied Doctor Stewart, one of the Red Cross officers, 'you can have it if you like, but I warn you that it is all wet with white paint'. His action was more than justified afterwards by the magnificent performance of *Number Four*, as the new train was called, for the wounded in South Africa.

The first Red Cross organization in the country was established at Pretoria on New Year's Day 1898; but in Cape Town 'The Good Hope Society for Aid to the Sick and Wounded in War' was created with the help of the British Red Cross, the two societies working side by side tending British and Boer wounded alike.

Britain had not been engaged in a major conflict for forty-five years when the South African war broke out on 11th October 1899; but her Red Cross society had been active on several occasions since its first undertakings in the Franco-Prussian war. Between 1876 and 1898 the society equipped ambulances and sent surgeons to work on the battlefields of Turkey, Bulgaria, Serbia, Greece and other countries. 'It would have been difficult for foreigners to do more and we can only admire the generosity, the energy and the administrative ability which the English Red Cross society displayed on these sad occasions,' Moynier had written.

Shortly before the outbreak of the South African War the British Red Cross was officially recognized by the War Office, thus realizing another of Dunant's aims, that of the voluntary aid society and the War Department working together. The society's pioneering days, when surgeons improvised operating theatres on the battlefield, were over; henceforth, its work was to supplement that of the Army Medical Services.

Meanwhile, on a December morning in 1901, a telegram arrived at the District Hospital in Heiden informing Dunant that he had been awarded a half-share in the first Nobel Peace Prize. Among the many messages of homage was one from the Society for Public Welfare in Geneva saying, 'There is no man who more deserves this honour'. He was not well enough to travel to Christiania, as Oslo was then known, to receive the Prize and was allowed to appoint a proxy.

Yet one thing more remained to place his memorial for ever among the fighting men on the battlefield, in war at sea and taken captive. The cause of which over the years he had been the champion was won six years later, when the Regulations annexed to the Hague Convention of 18th October 1907 Concerning the Laws and Customs of War on Land and at Sea gave prisoners of war rights and a status for the first time in history.

Dunant died at Heiden on 30th October 1910, at the age of eighty-two. It was his wish that no ceremony or publicity should surround his death; nor have they in the years since. It is the anniversary of his birth, 8th May, which is observed each year as 'World Red Cross, Red Crescent and Red Lion and Sun Day'.

5
V.A.D.

'Relief societies for the purpose of having care given to the wounded in wartime by ... thoroughly qualified volunteers ... organized and ready for the possibility of war,' were what Henri Dunant had advocated in *A Memory of Solferino*.

Since 1863 the formation of national societies had made rapid progress and by the closing years of the century over twenty-nine countries had established them. Women as well as men took to heart Dunant's words and prepared in time of peace and quiet for the work that would be expected of them in the event of war. The participation of women was one of the most interesting facts about the development of the Red Cross movement. Although at first they were excluded from some of the societies, they were admitted to several of the older ones and in Italy, Austria and Germany were on the administrative bodies. In Holland nursing instruction was given to all those who were willing to place themselves at the service of the Red Cross. In Germany, Sweden and Denmark they were specially trained for duties in hospitals and ambulances, though 'the work of transport, requiring much strength and activity' was considered 'out of the question' for them. In Russia, too, women were learning simple nursing to fit them for service with the Red Cross in war. In Berne the Swiss Red Cross established its first training school for nurses, who were to serve 'in places where the Red Cross is totally un-known'.

At one time the recruitment of nurses had presented special difficulties in Japan, where the idea of a woman looking after a man outside her family circle went against social custom and no woman of any standing could become a nurse without losing her reputation. But by the turn of the century the prejudice had largely been over-come and many women of the Japanese aristocracy were setting an example by becoming Red Cross nurses.

In some countries men also received simple instruction in nursing. The subject was included in the curricula of training for stretcher-bearers at the well-known centres established at Lille and Karlsruhe.

In Germany firemen and the members of the numerous gymnastic societies which were so popular throughout the country were encouraged to learn stretcher-bearing. Only men of robust health were accepted for the work and, it was emphasised, they must be of good moral character. At Stockholm young men called 'Volunteers' received a two-year training, at the end of which they were required to pass examinations in elementary anatomy, physiology and surgery as well as sick nursing. During annual army manoeuvres in Sweden, France and Italy, Red Cross members tried out the new first aid, stretcher-bearing and field-hospital equipment which was being developed.

Several of the societies carried the training of their volunteers a stage further and gave them the opportunity of gaining useful practical experience for their wartime work by undertaking relief for the victims of famine, epidemics, shipwreck, fire, earthquakes and other disas-ters. But, it was stressed, by stepping out of their normal sphere of duties they could not demand the services of foreign societies. An early example of international Red Cross aid to the victims of natural disaster was provided, characteristically, by the American Red Cross. In 1891 when famine swept Russia and the Russian Red Cross was called to help in the stricken areas, thousands of bushels of corn and pounds of flour were sent to Russia by the American Red Cross.

Clara Barton, the society's president, had already organized relief for flood victims and collected money and gifts for the homeless after a cyclone in the United States, proving that the Red Cross was not only an auxiliary to the army in war-time but an aid to the government in time of peace.

By 1900 the Italian Red Cross had implemented an anti-malaria campaign for workers throughout the Roman countryside, where the fever was especially severe among the inhabitants who slept in the open air. In Germany the Red Cross was chosen as the official organization to help the health authorities in the fight against tuberculosis and established a number of sanatoria. Following the example of the French and British societies, the Uruguayan Red Cross set up relief posts for shipwreck victims at danger points along the coast.

After the Franco-Prussian war, part of the surplus funds collected by the British Red Cross was used to pay for the training of nurses at the Royal Victoria Hospital at Netley. The society had never lacked volunteers when they were needed, and it was not until the passing of the Territorial and Reserve Forces Act of 1907 that a permanent body, trained in peace to be ready for war, came into being. The act was brought in at a time when the growth in German armaments was becoming a threat to

Britain's security. The British Red Cross was called upon to recruit and train men and women to supplement the medical services of the Territorial forces in the event of war, and responded by forming Voluntary Aid Detachments composed of men trained in first aid, and women in first aid and auxiliary nursing.

The Polytechnic Institute has the distinction of forming the first Voluntary Aid Detachments of the British Red Cross Society. London/1 was recruited from the students attending an ambulance class for men at the Institute in 1909; London/2, a women's detachment, was formed five months later. It was decided that these two detachments must prove their worth before others were raised. They won their laurels the following year at a display in the White City Stadium, where they greatly impressed the spectators by their ingenious improvisations of equipment for use in war. A two-wheeled country car was converted into an ambulance (ambulances were horse-drawn vehicles in those days), stretchers were made from pitch-fork handles and straw rope twisted on the spot, and then converted into beds by attaching them to spade-handles for bedposts, which raised them off the ground. Tents and shelters were also improvised.

The training proved useful to the London/1 members who served as a Red Cross unit in Montenegro during the war with Turkey in 1912. The detachment was the first to be called up for duty when the First World War broke out two years later. The following year some of the members were entrusted with conveying King George V from Victoria Station to Buckingham Palace when he returned from the front after his severe accident.

The initials 'V.A.D.' soon came to be applied to the man or woman who, in fact, was a member of a Volun-

FRANCE
ITALY
MALTA
GIBRA
SALON

EGYPT
MESOPOTAMIA
HOLLAND
SWITZERLAND
RUSSIA

V.A.D.

NURSING MEMBERS . COOKS, KITCHEN-MAIDS
CLERKS , HOUSE-MAIDS , WARD-MAIDS,
LAUNDRESSES, MOTOR-DRIVERS. ETC:

ARE URGENTLY NEEDED

APPLICATION TO BE MADE TO

tary Aid Detachment. The term became so famous in the 1914–18 war that it added a new word to the English language. As more men were called up for service with the armed forces the letters were more closely associated with women—the girls in the light blue dresses and crisp white aprons with a red cross on the bib. Although over the years the uniform of the women V.A.D.s has undergone several changes, basically it has remained the same and is probably best known as the uniform of the British Red Cross society.

The work of these V.A.D.s was one of the outstanding features of the First World War and proved what women were capable of doing. Those were the days before jobs for women were taken as a matter of course, and when the need for their services arose they gave up the sheltered life and protection of their homes and flocked to offer themselves for duties with the Red Cross. By October 1914 the first sixteen of them, under two trained nurses, had been mobilized for foreign service and started a Rest Station near Boulogne. Before the war ended women V.A.D.s were to be found in France, Flanders, Serbia, Montenegro, Malta, Italy, Russia, Romania, Mesopotamia, North Persia and East Africa; working in military and Red Cross hospitals, on hospital barges, in hostels, rest stations and when the supply of men began to run short, employed as ambulance drivers.

Motor-ambulances, replacing the horse-drawn vehicles hitherto used for conveying the wounded, were among the many revolutionary changes of the war. They were introduced by the British Red Cross in 1915 and with

A recruitment poster for V.A.D.s, painted by
Mrs Joyce Dennys in 1918

A German prisoner of war having his hand dressed by a British V.A.D. at Abbeville, 1917

such success that the War Office immediately began organizing convoys of them. The first to be taken over by V.A.D. women drivers was in April a year later; within the next two years they were serving with thirty-three ambulance units in France.

These women were not lightly described as 'heroines of the war'. Cars not being then what they are now, their drivers were subject to constant nerve strain; engines had to be cranked and broken wrists were a common occurrence. It was all part of the normal duty of a V.A.D. in cold weather to get up every two hours during the night to start up the cars so that they would be ready for an emergency.

The First World War showed a vast expansion in the work of the Red Cross. All the belligerents had well-organized national societies, which gave their full support to the military authorities by establishing hospitals and providing ambulances, equipment and personnel.

The responsibilities of the International Committee were greatly increased. The Hague Regulations of 1907, making official provisions for prisoners of war, gave the Committee a legal justification for its many services to them. Article 14 of the Regulations, under which an official enquiry bureau for prisoners was to be instituted in each State, especially concerned the Red Cross, which established in Geneva a Central Agency of Information to which the belligerents sent lists of their captives and other data about them.

The war was fought on a scale unapproached in any former century, leaving behind it a corresponding measure of suffering and distress. When hostilities ended, the national societies not only gave relief to sick and disabled ex-servicemen and the widows and dependents of men killed in action, but also cared for injured and

V.A.D. women drivers running to their ambulances, 1917

homeless civilians of towns and villages which had been destroyed in the fighting.

In the immediate post-war years the Red Cross accomplished tasks whose scope ranged far beyond care of the sick and wounded. In 1919 twenty-six national societies helped the International Committee to carry out in Eastern Europe an extensive anti-typhus campaign, during which an American Red Cross anti-typhus train travelled back and forth saving lives across more than four thousand miles of Siberia. In 1921 large-scale relief operations were undertaken for the victims of famine in Russia and the millions of refugees who left the country to escape the effects of hunger and the revolution.

The end of the war also saw the establishment of the Junior Red Cross movement.

When Mrs Eleanor Mackinnon began forming her Red Cross circles among the school children of Sydney, Australia in 1914, she little imagined they were to be the nucleus of the Junior Red Cross, which has since spread from country to country, attracting millions of boys and girls to join it in subsequent years.

Throughout the history of the Red Cross children had helped it in practical ways on numerous occasions, and the idea of allowing them to become members had been seriously considered in Spain as early as 1896. During the Franco-Prussian war French school-children made bandages and dressings for the wounded; in 1885, four years after Clara Barton had founded the American Red Cross, she received fifty-one dollars, raised by some children in Pennsylvania for the victims of the Ohio River floods; with the donation the children had written, 'Some time again when you want money to help you in your good work, call on *The Little Six*'. Their contribution was put towards buying a small house for the mother and orphaned children of one of the flood victims and named after their young benefactors. American children had also helped their mothers to prepare relief material for San Francisco after the earthquake which destroyed the city in 1906. 'The Maple Leaf Club', formed in a school in Saskatchewan, worked for the Red Cross throughout the South African war; so it was scarcely surprising that Canada should follow Australia's example by forming junior groups in 1915. When the United States entered the war in 1917, President Woodrow Wilson himself recommended the idea to the American Red Cross as a way in which young people could help in meeting national needs.

Mrs Mackinnon established her Junior Red Cross circles in Australia on the ideals of the parent society. She worked out a practical programme, which enabled the children to help those who were wounded or in other ways affected by the war, and which included learning first aid, life-saving and camp-cooking. Service for others was the keynote of her junior movement then, as it is now. By 1918 a large number of school circles had been formed in Australia and the juniors embarked upon the first of their post-war ventures, raising money to furnish and equip 'Blinded Soldiers' Tearooms'. They next turned their attention to helping the sick children of invalid ex-servicemen: in 1924 a house called 'Shuna' was lent to the Australian juniors, and six little girls suffering from tuberculosis were installed in it under the care of a matron until they recovered; shortly afterwards a similar home, 'Juong', was opened for soldiers' sons. These houses were the first preventoria to be established in Australia.

In 1918 many children in the war-stricken countries were ill and hungry, orphaned and homeless, and the American juniors opened their Red Cross National Children's Fund for them. Supplies of clothing were sent to meet their immediate needs and not long afterwards the first of the Gift Boxes, which American juniors have continued to send to sick and needy children when the occasion has called for them.

A new chapter opened in the history of the Red Cross movement about this time; largely through the initiative of Mr Henry P. Davison, the chairman of the American Red Cross. The way in which the national societies had worked together to relieve the suffering caused by the war had so impressed him that he felt the spirit of unity should be preserved. At his suggestion the League of Red Cross Societies was created, linking the national societies in an association to work for 'the improvement of health, the prevention of disease and the mitigation of suffering throughout the world'.

On 5th May 1919, representatives of the Red Cross societies of France, Great Britain, Italy, Japan and the United States met in Paris to inaugurate the League, which, ever since, has played a prominent part in the international work of the movement. The League's principal functions are to assist in the formation and development of new societies and to co-ordinate Red Cross relief activities, especially for the victims of disaster.

Its foundation and the introduction of peacetime purposes for the Red Cross considerably enlarged the scope of the national societies, bringing fresh tasks and opening up wider horizons to them.

Two years later, one of the greatest humanitarian services to mankind was started at a Red Cross centre in

Talfourd Road, Camberwell, London. Mr Percy Lane Oliver and his British Red Cross V.A.D.s were holding a meeting when the telephone rang. It was King's College Hospital, who asked for a blood donor. Mr Oliver hesitated a moment. 'We are all working men and women here—' he began doubtfully. But when the hospital explained that it would not take long he put it to the others; he would go for one, he said, and all of them volunteered. The selected donor, a woman, gave her blood without any detrimental effects to herself; the patient's life was saved.

The incident was to start the first voluntary blood donor service in the world.

The V.A.D'.s example gave Mr Oliver the idea of forming a panel of donors to supply blood, by day or night, to any London hospital. In time the panel became the Greater London Red Cross Blood Transfusion Service and it was taken over by the British Red Cross in 1926.

The panel of donors has about two thousand names on it and the service is conducted on very personal lines; the donor afterwards receiving a report describing the outcome of the case for which the blood was required. Although science has enabled blood to be stored for a time before being used, fresh blood is needed in many of the operations now made possible by the tremendous advances in surgery and anaesthesia; and the donor who enrols with the Greater London Red Cross service has the satisfaction of knowing that the blood is being given to someone in vital need.

In 1935 the British Red Cross was called upon by the government to undertake responsibility for the public's safety in the event of another war, and began training its members in Air Raid Precautions. All too soon the letters

'A.R.P.' were to assume their sinister implication throughout the United Kingdom. For the present, the necessity for studying these safeguards seemed remote enough to the man in the street, even when he opened his newspaper in the autumn of that year and read of the Italian invasion of Abyssinia and mass raids on civilians, hospitals and ambulances.

The British Red Cross sent two ambulance units to Abyssinia, the Italians having declined the offer of help as they had ample resources. Reports from Doctor Macfie, a member of one British Red Cross unit, told of men, women and children horribly burned by mustard gas. The other unit suffered the tragic loss of its leader, Doctor John Melly, who was shot by a bandit when he went to the aid of a woman wounded in the streets of Addis Ababa and died as the Italians were entering the city at the end of the war.

The Red Cross societies of Sweden, Holland, Norway, Finland and the Egyptian Red Crescent sent ambulance units to Abyssinia.

Delegates of the International Committee of the Red Cross were also sent there; for one of them Abyssinia proved to be the first of many missions he was to undertake for the Committee.

6
A Delegate of the International Committee

One day in the autumn of 1935 a young Swiss doctor in the last year of his resident training at a hospital near Mulhouse was called to the telephone. He recognized the voice of a friend whom he knew to be working with the International Committee of the Red Cross in Geneva.

The Committee were urgently needing a doctor to send to Abyssinia; would he agree to go, the friend asked, and added that he must have an answer before the day was out.

That telephone call for Marcel Junod was the beginning of a story of devoted and courageous service to the Red Cross, which took him from Abyssinia to Spain, Germany, Poland, France, England, Turkey, Greece, Persia and Russia and, finally, across Siberia through Manchuria to China and Japan, where he was among the first to visit Hiroshima after the nuclear bomb had destroyed it in 1945.

He later described some of his experiences as a delegate of the International Committee of the Red Cross in a book entitled *Warrior Without Weapons*, in which he wrote:

'There are never more than two adversaries engaged in battle. But these adversaries are apt to find that suddenly in their midst is a third combatant—a warrior without weapons.'

In these few words he defined a delegate of the International Committee in war, and at his death on 16th June 1961, all who knew him felt he could have no more suitable epitaph.

From Mulhouse Doctor Junod went first to the Committee's headquarters at the Villa Moynier in Geneva, where he spent the next few weeks studying maps and preparing for his mission to Abyssinia. As he was sitting in the library one morning poring over the texts of the Geneva Conventions, he was joined by another of the delegates.

'Books are all very well,' the other remarked, catching sight of what Doctor Junod was reading, 'but when you're on the spot, thousands of miles from Geneva, all on your own, you'll have to fall back on your imagination. There are the official Red Cross texts, of course, but, above all, there's the spirit of the thing.'

Time and again in his service with the Red Cross Doctor Junod was to realize the truth of those words. Within weeks he was to see the Red Cross emblem riddled with bullets and shattered by bombs on plain and hillside; he was also to see the invincible spirit of the men who worked on in its name long after its emblem had ceased to protect them.

When he arrived in Addis Ababa the situation was discouraging. The shortage of medical personnel was acute. There was only one Abyssinian doctor in the country, a few foreign doctors in private practice who had expressed their willingness to work for the Red Cross, and a few hospitals run by foreign missionaries in the larger towns such as Dessie. The Emperor's troops were going into battle without doctors, nurses or even bandages; whether or not anything could be done about it depended entirely on the Red Cross.

In the offices of the newly-formed Abyssinian society he took stock of the situation: the foreign Red Cross ambulance units which had arrived in the country were well-equipped and the best of their kind; the Abyssinian Red Cross had managed to form two and purchase enough supplies to fit out ten; within the next few days they made up four more units, each in the charge of a foreign doctor, and set out for the various battlefronts.

Disturbing news reached Doctor Junod not long afterwards. Dessie, which had been declared an open town, had been heavily bombed by Italian planes on 6th December; the hospital had been hit and some of the Red Cross ambulances destroyed. He decided to go there immediately to see for himself the extent of the damage.

The young Greek surgeon in charge of the first Abyssinian unit, who met him at Dessie, told him all that had happened. It seemed scarcely possible that the Italians could have made a mistake; even if they had failed to see the Red Cross flags flying over the tents, they could hardly have missed seeing the huge red cross painted on the hospital roof. Besides which, the attack had been carried out in broad daylight and continued for about an hour.

There had been no mistake. The destruction was intended, and all the doctors signed a letter of protest and sent it to the League of Nations. The result for the Red Cross ambulances was disastrous. The Swedish unit operating at Sidamo—the only source of medical aid for the entire Abyssinian southern army—was destroyed next, followed by attacks on the second of the Abyssinian units under the care of an Austrian doctor, and finally a British Red Cross unit.

As Doctor Junod looked round at the scattered remains of the Swedish ambulance he caught sight of a scrap of paper, part of the wrapping round a packet of dressings, on which were printed the word 'Stockholm' and a red cross—the sign that had led men to journey thousands of miles to an unknown land to help strangers in distress.

The rules laid down by the Geneva Convention had been faithfully observed by the ambulances; the tents sufficiently far removed from any military objective, and clearly identified by the Red Cross flags flying above them and spread out over the ground around them. But the repeated attacks on the units showed that the emblem afforded them no protection; and first one unit then another removed all signs of it, and continued their work under cover of trees or camouflaged.

The Italians' intention was proved beyond all doubt shortly afterwards, when leaflets printed in Amharic were dropped over parts of the country, informing the people that they must expect reprisals if they violated international law by capturing Italian pilots and cutting off their heads. One Italian airman had been beheaded after making a forced landing behind the Abyssinian lines.

The two Polish doctors attached to the Abyssinian ambulance on the northern front were then captured by the Italians, who heaped reproaches on them for serving with the Negus and writing in protest to the League of Nations. They were tortured and thrown into prison. After this the Greek surgeon was reported missing, probably dead, and one of the doctors attached to the

Netherlands unit disappeared. It was later discovered that he had been captured by Chiftas, the Abyssinian bandits who roamed the countryside mysteriously armed with new Italian rifles, menacing the population behind the army lines.

Doctor Junod narrowly escaped with his life on several occasions. The plane with its red cross markings, which took him to the various places where the ambulances were stationed, was repeatedly attacked by the Italians and destroyed on an airfield. When Addis Ababa fell, looting and plundering broke out all over the city; bands of Chiftas swarmed through it; shops, warehouses and private houses were broken into and set alight by drunken mobs, who fired on the inhabitants, killing and wounding them in the streets.

People who could find cellars took refuge in them, barricading the entrances with anything they could lay hands on. It was from the basement of a house in the centre of the city as the Italians were entering it, that Doctor Junod was eventually rescued and conducted to the French Embassy and safety.

When he arrived back at the International Committee's headquarters to give his report on the nine months he had spent in Abyssinia, he found the members earnestly discussing the situation in Spain, where civil war had broken out in July. With his recent experience, he was clearly the most suitable person to tackle the new problem.

The International Committee's task in Spain was entirely different from that in Abyssinia. The Geneva Conventions provided no regulations for the victims of civil wars; the Committee's power lay in 'the spirit of the thing' and not by right of the written texts.

The cruellest aspect of the Spanish civil war, which was to last for two and a half years, was the taking and shooting of hostages by the two opposing sides, the Nationalists and the Republicans. Men and women were removed from their homes and disappeared without a trace; even children were not spared and hundreds of them were seized and held by their enemies. The Spanish gaols were full of so-called political prisoners, some of whom had the misfortune to be condemned to the holds of prisonships, where the conditions resembled those of the hulks of bygone days.

If, through the intervention of the International Committee of the Red Cross, a stop could be put to the hideous practice of taking hostages, and prisoners of both sides could be exchanged, thousands of Spanish lives would

Refugees of the Spanish Civil War (1936–1939) at Hendaye Plage. Many Spanish refugees were placed in camps in France, where they remained throughout the Second World War

be saved. Although Spain had a long established Red Cross Society (it was founded in 1864), by now it had been stripped of much of its authority and divided by its countrymen; only a neutral intermediary could hope to avert the needless loss of life.

Doctor Junod's first action was to persuade the two sides to agree to an exchange of prisoners. He began with two hostages who were awaiting execution: Don Esteban of Bilbao, put forward by the Republicans to be exchanged for the socialist Mayor of Bilbao, a prisoner of the Nationalists. On the success of this venture depended all his future attempts to effect exchanges.

The arrangements had taken a great deal of time; the heavy fighting made it almost impossible to cross from one side of Spain to the other; it was quicker to leave the country and re-enter it by sea or across the nearest frontier when he wished to interview Republicans or Nationalists. Since the actual exchange could not be carried out on Spanish soil, it was arranged that it should take place at an hotel in the little French town of St Jean-de-Luz.

Filled with gratitude towards the Republicans for setting an example by releasing Don Esteban, Doctor Junod escorted him to the hotel and started out for the Nationalist headquarters at Pamplona to collect the Mayor.

But a bitter disappointment awaited him. The order for the release of the Mayor had been countermanded, and at the prison the governor refused to hand him over. Doctor Junod spent the day frantically telephoning one authority then another until, after hours of waiting, he at last obtained a personal order from General Mola, collected his prisoner and drove off with him to St Jean-de-Luz. In the hotel lounge the two Spaniards embraced each other affectionately; both of them saved, through the intervention of the Red Cross, from the death to which their own countrymen had condemned them. The success of Doctor Junod's venture became known and hundreds of people came to see him and implored him to continue his efforts.

The Republicans made the next move, agreeing to release a hundred and thirty women and girls in exchange for the same number of Basque women held by the Nationalists. A British destroyer, H.M.S. *Exmouth*, conveyed them to St Jean-de-Luz where they were disembarked, taken across the frontier to San Sebastian and reunited with their families. But when Doctor Junod asked for the Basque women who were to be handed over to him, he met with a blank refusal. Several weeks of negotiations followed, but he failed to obtain their release; instead, he succeeded in extracting a promise from the Nationalists that forty Basque children who had been captured while on holiday near Burgos, should be returned to their parents, and sent a telegram informing the Republicans. *Exmouth* was to take the children aboard at St Jean-de-Luz and transport them to Bilbao.

On the morning of their departure Doctor Junod waited at the appointed meeting-place. Time went on; no children appeared. The Nationalists had again broken their word; the order for the children's release had been countermanded. Disgusted by the Nationalists' treachery and beside himself with grief, he boarded the destroyer and returned to Bilbao to explain to the parents what had happened.

As *Exmouth* entered the roads he could hear the church bells and see the crowds swarming on the quay to greet the children. As he stepped down the gangway the mothers surrounded him. 'But the children?' they asked bewildered, 'where are our children?'

At one time they had expected never to see their children again; now, he had been the cause of raising their hopes only to dash them. Overcome by the disappointment some turned angry and spat in his face, accusing the Red Cross of having deceived them. Shouts and abuse followed Doctor Junod as he made his way to address the gathering of people at the town centre where, once more, he solemnly promised them the return of their children within the next ten days.

By now some of the Nationalists were beginning to understand the humanitarian purposes of his work. Even so, his renewed attempt to obtain the children's release proved as difficult as his former had been and was not made easier by the time-limit he had set himself.

Nevertheless, the joyful scenes were repeated in Bilbao ten days later. *Exmouth* steamed into port and this time she was indeed bringing the children home.

As the days lengthened into weeks and months the exchange of lives went on. The lists of those put forward for exchange grew longer until, one day, there were two thousand names.

Other delegates of the International Committee had by now joined Doctor Junod. They visited the prisoners in the gaols and interceded first with one side, then the other, to allow the exchanges and personally supervised and carried through each operation. Often their efforts were made on behalf of men condemned to die within a few hours, and in the short while that remained before sentence was carried out the delegates travelled great distances in a race against time to reach the particular official who had the power to rescind the order.

For the thousands of people whose relatives had disappeared and from whom nothing had been heard, the delegates devised the Spanish Family News service and persuaded the two sides to allow them to operate it. The service consisted of the transmission of a card bearing a name, an address, a message of twenty-five words and a signature; sometimes the censor had deleted so many words that only the signature remained, but the card was greeted with tears of joy by the imprisoned man's family.

Five million of these Red Cross cards were exchanged between the two fighting sides before the war in Spain finally came to an end with the surrender of Madrid on 30th March 1939.

Even before the Spanish Civil War had ended other events were occupying the attention of the Red Cross. It was becoming clear that Nazi Germany would not long delay another crisis which must lead to war.

All through August 1939 tension mounted between Germany and Poland. At dawn on 1st September Poland was invaded. Britain and France declared war on Germany two days later.

A second World War had been started. The torch lit on the frontiers of eastern Europe was rapidly to set the whole world aflame.

7

For Those Behind Barbed Wire

During the six unhappy years of the Second World War it is difficult to imagine what it would have been like without the Red Cross. The war was a 'total war', in which civilians were exposed to the same risks and suffered as much, and even more, than the armed forces. There were few countries which escaped the conflict.

The conquest of Poland was followed elsewhere by a period of comparative quiet known as the 'phoney war'. But in the early spring of 1940 fighting broke out in earnest, with the lightning invasion and occupation of one country after another. Heavy air raids destroyed towns and cities, causing severe casualties among civilians, thousands of whom fled from their homes to seek refuge in other countries, only to be caught up later by the enemy advance. In the countries under German occupation, the misery of the people was intensified by mass deportations to provide workers for the slave labour systems, the use of concentration camps, the atrocities committed in them and the extermination of some six million Jews.

In the midst of the despair and suffering there was the Red Cross; its ideals contained in a great treaty signed by all the nations which was not allowed to lapse after they had gone to war; and where this formal agreement was deficient the Red Cross, which had the power to influence world opinion so greatly, brought its influence to bear and succeeded in lessening many of the cruelties of war.

Ten years before the outbreak of war, the Hague Regulations of 1907 concerning the treatment of prisoners of war had been revised and considerably extended. Experience gained in the First World War of 1914-18 had shown them to be inadequate in a number of respects, and the seventeen articles of the original text were expanded in the Geneva Convention of 1929, to no fewer than ninety-seven; most of them concerned with safeguarding a prisoner's rights and the obligations of those who held him captive.

In 1914 the International Committee of the Red Cross had set up an inquiry bureau for prisoners of war; by the terms of the 1929 Convention it was officially authorized to do so. The Central Agency for Prisoners of War was housed in one of the largest buildings in Geneva where, under a vast card index system, were assembled, in alphabetical order, the names and particulars of prisoners of war, interned civilians and missing servicemen.

Between April and June 1940 events in Europe moved fast. German troops invaded and occupied Denmark and Norway, and in May, Holland, Belgium and Luxembourg; strong armoured divisions broke through the Allied line along the Belgian frontier and rapidly overran France which, on 22nd June, signed an armistice with Germany. Meanwhile, Italy had entered the war on the side of her Axis partner and the famous evacuation of British and Allied troops from the Dunkirk beaches had been accomplished.

Although a large part of the British army was successfully brought back to England—the epic of 'the Little Ships' is written in the pages of history—some forty thousand men were left behind as prisoners of war and for a time listed as missing. The Central Agency in Geneva, which received the earliest notification of a prisoner's capture through the official lists sent to it by the belligerents, was flooded with inquiries from next of kin.

Under the terms of the Convention every prisoner of war was allowed to send news of his capture to his next of kin within a week of his arrival at a prison camp or hospital. When the news was received at the Central Agency, the information was recorded on a coloured 'Capture Card'—different colours being used for the cards of the different nationalities—and filed. Any inquiry from his next of kin had meanwhile been noted on a white 'Tally Card' and joined the other white cards in an index. By a special mechanical process called a 'concordance' the Capture Card and Tally Card would meet to give proof of the man's capture; but not until the two cards had met was the relative's inquiry answered.

An extraordinary situation developed in the section at the Agency where the cards had been filed for close on a million French prisoners of war, who had remained in German hands under the terms of the Franco-German armistice. It was not they who were missing but their next of kin. In their chaotic flight to escape the German advance, the families had taken to the roads bound for the south and for a time all trace of them was lost.

The greatest care was needed in recording, checking and filing the names at the Agency, to avoid any possibility of sending wrong information. To guard against mistakes when replying to enquiries for men who bore the same name was a constant anxiety. The Agency's files contained no fewer than fifteen thousand cards for 'Martin', fourteen hundred of them with the christian name of 'Jean'; in the British section were forty-five thousand for 'Smith'. Finding the man whose card had been filed under the wrong section because of the different ways in which his name had been spelt could entail hours of searching: HATSIANAGNOSTOU, HADZIANGNOSTOU, HADJIANSNOSTOU and HASSIANGNOSTOU were not four people, but four variations in the spelling of the same Greek sailor's name.

When a man was reported missing the International Committee set to work as thoroughly as any detective, piecing together every scrap of information and following up every clue which might lead to finding him. The discovery of one member of a crew or unit often led to finding out the fate of the rest. Prisoners known to be in the same regiment, air or ship's crew as a missing man would be questioned; the mayor of a town in or near which fighting had taken place, priests, schoolmasters and anyone in authority would be drawn into the search for him.

On one occasion a prisoner, replying to an inquiry about a missing companion, said he had been killed in action and was buried near a baker's shop in a town in northern France. He had no idea of the name of the shop, but if he saw it again he was sure he would recognize it. The International Committee promptly wrote to the mayor of the town, who replied sending photographs of several bakers' shops. From these the prisoner was able to pick out the bakery near which his companion's grave was found.

Of all the services carried out by the Red Cross in the war none appealed more to the public imagination than the provision of parcels, especially food parcels, for prisoners of war. To many people it was the most important of the Red Cross functions, and donations poured in for the purpose.

Parcels for British prisoners were packed in Canada and New Zealand as well as in the United Kingdom, where the first packing-centre was opened in St James's Palace in November 1939, and nineteen other centres were set up in various parts of the country before the end of the war.

The Geneva Convention made provision for prisoners to receive food in addition to that supplied by their captors; and without it their health, especially during a long captivity, would undoubtedly have suffered. 'The parcels saved our lives!' was a phrase which occurred repeatedly in letters from prisoners in the camps and after their return home.

The arrival of the parcels at the camps produced feelings of well-being and contentment among the men, and the thrill of 'parcels day' never quite wore off even after two or three years in captivity.

In the beginning British prisoners were so few that the parcels were addressed to them individually; but with the steep rise in numbers after the fall of France they were consigned to the International Committee in Geneva for distribution to the camps.

In getting the parcels to Geneva the British Red Cross faced numerous difficulties, the chief of which was in finding a settled route for them. At first the parcels had gone through Belgium, and after the German occupation France and Switzerland; with the fall of France they were sent through Portugal, Spain and for a time un-occupied France, until at last a route for them was found via Lisbon and Marseilles. But the ships which carried them were exposed to all the normal war risks of vessels on the high seas and often bombed or torpedoed. From time to time the packages were pilfered on their journeys and the climax was reached when some thousands of parcels were lost somewhere between Britain and Geneva.

In the camps the prisoners waited and watched anxiously for their arrival.

There was only one solution to the problem and it was suggested by Doctor Junod: the International Committee of the Red Cross must charter its own ships to carry the parcels safely across the seas. It was an ambitious project, but the German naval authorities gave their consent to it provided that the British Admiralty also agreed. The reply to the proposal sent to London was, however, an emphatic 'No'.

Doctor Junod decided to go to London to discuss the matter with the Admiralty. He was accompanied by Mademoiselle Odier, who was wholeheartedly for the plan. She had worked for the International Committee for many years and during the First World War all foreign soldiers who were interned in Geneva had come under her care. She had organized relief in the Spanish civil war, providing food and clothing for the victims when the situation had been at its worst.

At the Admiralty the delegates were met by the First Lord's secretary to whom Mademoiselle Odier explained the purpose of their visit. She pleaded with him for the Allied prisoners, who far outnumbered the British and Commonwealth, and told him of the piteous state of the civilians in war-torn Poland and Greece. The ships, she explained, carrying the supplies they so desperately needed could not by the rules of international law use the same markings as those for hospital ships; something entirely new had been devised. If the Admiralty would agree to the plan the International Committee would take full responsibility for carrying it out.

The Naval officer rose and left the room; thousands of lives depended upon the answer he brought back from beyond the door he shut so firmly behind him. The delegates waited. As the hands of the clock on the chimney-piece moved towards the half hour, the officer rejoined them and they knew from the expression on his face that their errand had not been in vain.

The Red Cross was to write a page in naval history. While Europe met blockade with counter-blockade, a body of private citizens was to bring food and other supplies into the beleaguered continent.

Before long the ships, with the word 'C-International' painted in bold letters along their sides, and the red cross emblem displayed on their bows and top deck illuminated at night, were sailing openly across the Atlantic and through the Mediterranean with their

A 'C-International' ship. The Second World War led to the establishment, in 1942, of the Foundation for the Organization of Red Cross Transports, with a fleet of twelve vessels

precious cargoes destined for prisoners and starving people in Europe. The privilege carried enormous responsibilities with it. The exact time the ships put to sea had to be communicated to all belligerents and safe-conducts obtained for the vessels well in advance of their sailings. They were neutral ships, manned by neutral crews, and a representative of the International Committee travelled on every voyage. He checked the loading and unloading of the cargo and made sure that only Red Cross supplies and the ship's crew were on board. It was imperative that these rules should be honourably observed since the power of the Red Cross rested on good faith, and its emblem could never be used in any way to deceive those who had put their trust in it.

The ships carried not only food for the prisoners but invalid and medical supplies, clothing, comforts, games, musical instruments and parcels from their next-of-kin. There were parcels containing seeds so that the prisoners could cultivate flowers and grow vegetables to vary the monotony of their diet. There were books of all kinds and, for the camps in Germany, educational materials. Requests for books from prisoners who wished to study special subjects were many, ranging from Chinese porcelain to baking 'white, brown, smalls, rolls and all classes of buns and cakes', from boot-repairing to gold-mining.

With the help of the Red Cross Educational Books scheme thousands of prisoners returned from captivity better equipped to take up careers for which they had qualified at the 'Barbed Wire Universities'. The examinations held in the camps were conducted with full formalities and the papers sent home for marking. Many prisoners of war passed university examinations leading to degrees, and in no case was the standard of the papers lowered because they were prisoners. German and Italian prisoners of war in Allied hands also received parcels, as their countries had signed and ratified the Geneva Convention of 1929.

The International Committee's delegates inspected the prisoner of war camps from time to time and their reports were submitted to the prisoners' own governments and the detaining powers. The visits brought the delegates into personal contact with the prisoners, who were allowed to make complaints to them if anything was wrong, and if justified to have it put right.

But the Red Cross was powerless to help Russian prisoners in the hands of the Axis Powers and Axis nationals detained in the U.S.S.R. Neither Russia nor Finland had ratified the 1929 Convention; even so, there was nothing to prevent either country when it entered the war from observing the treaty in practice. Finland, indeed, was willing to implement the terms. The International Committee offered its services to all belligerents whether or not they had ratified the Convention; but despite repeated attempts, it failed to open up negotiations with the two main adversaries, Germany and Russia, on the subject of their prisoners.

It was immediately after Doctor Junod had visited a prisoner of war camp for British officers in Germany that he came face to face with a living example of the fate of captives who had been denied the benefits of the Convention and the services which the Red Cross extended to all war victims.

On a wall of the hut in which he met the British prisoners was the text of the treaty which gave them the right to receive parcels, letters from home, cigarettes and other comforts; let alone to complain that there were not enough shower-baths and wash-basins and that they needed more cupboards for their belongings. As Doctor Junod entered the hut he noticed cricket-bats, boxing-gloves, footballs, a gramophone and records; there were about four thousand books in the library, the Camp Officer told him, and a reserve of eighteen thousand Red Cross parcels in the store.

A few paces from these huts and separated from them by only a double line of barbed wire, was another group: a camp for Russian prisoners. At first the German officer had refused to allow Doctor Junod to visit it. As long as German prisoners in Soviet camps were denied visits from delegates of the International Committee, he reminded him, visits to Russian prisoners in German hands were forbidden. After some persuasion the officer relented, and allowed Doctor Junod to enter the camp provided that he carried out the inspection in absolute silence and made no official report on it.

As they approached the huts, a line of famished men shuffled past them; weak, ragged and dejected, they held out their battered tins and pannikins for a ladleful of watery soup, while a German guard, cracking a whip, shouted at them to keep moving. Inside the huts the walls were bare; the stove was cold and the prisoners slept on the floor without mattresses or even straw. No letters, no parcels, no hope could find a way into those huts. Meanwhile, long columns of German prisoners were dragging their way across Russia to camps in Siberia, where a similar fate awaited them.

Shortly after this experience, Doctor Junod began preparations for leaving Europe on his final mission, which was to take him to the Far East, where war had broken out on 7th December 1941 after Japan's sudden attack on Pearl Harbour, the American naval base in the Hawaiian Islands. Declarations of war on Britain and America had followed immediately.

During the next few months one disaster succeeded another for the Allies. Japan occupied Hong Kong, the Philippines and South Pacific islands and overran Burma, Malaya and Singapore.

Thousands of Allied prisoners fell into Japanese hands; thousands of civilians—men, women and children—were rounded up and put into internment camps. Japan had signed but not ratified the Geneva Convention of 1929 and was not, therefore, bound by its terms.

The Japanese government, however, gave an undertaking that it would observe the terms of the treaty *mutatis mutandis* (that is, with due alteration of details) with tragic consequences for the captives.

From Geneva, the International Committee appealed to Swiss doctors, missionaries, merchants and businessmen living in the Far East to become its delegates. Far away from Geneva, separated from each other by thousands of miles in these vast scattered territories and with no written texts to support their actions, these Swiss nationals accepted a thankless task which promised from the outset to require tact, resourcefulness and no little courage.

To be taken captive was a disgrace and a humiliation in the eyes of the Japanese; they themselves when taken prisoner neither asked for anything nor could understand why the Red Cross should show any interest in their fate. Their own people had no sympathy for them and none for enemy prisoners. This attitude accounted for much of the Japanese ill-treatment of the prisoners in their hands and the indifference with which they met the Red Cross delegates' requests to be allowed to visit the camps, operate a regular parcels service and postal message scheme. The existence of many of the camps was hidden from the delegates; they were allowed to carry out welfare work in only a private capacity and never succeeded in obtaining from the Japanese a complete list of the captives.

A few months after war had broken out with Japan, an exchange of diplomatists was carried out at Lourenço Marques, a neutral port in Portuguese East Africa, and the Japanese agreed to allow the returning ships to carry Red Cross supplies for the camps. When the captains announced their intention of sailing immediately the exchanges had been completed, the people of Lourenço Marques overwhelmed them with invitations to dinner-parties, receptions and other forms of entertainment to delay their departure. Meanwhile the South African Red Cross worked feverishly, loading up every corner of the ships' holds with parcels of food which had been rushed into the port.

But when the supplies arrived in the occupied territories, the Japanese authorities refused to allow the Red Cross delegates to handle them and themselves distributed them to the camps. Few prisoners received parcels spread out among so many.

After several attempts to establish a parcels service to the camps had failed, the Red Cross delegates devised an alternative plan, making 'local purchases' of food, medicines and other relief goods for the inmates of the camps. Interned civilians mainly benefited from the scheme which, although it could never take the place of regular issues of Red Cross parcels, provided the unfortunate captives with a few of the things they so badly needed.

The International Committee pressed its delegates to obtain individual receipts for the supplies which were delivered to the inmates at the camps. This practice had arisen when the Germans eventually agreed to allow Red Cross parcels, addressed directly to individuals by name, to be sent into the concentration camps. Some of the receipts came back to Geneva bearing not only the signature of the addressee but a list of names of fellow concentration camp victims to whom parcels could then be sent. The Japanese, unfortunately, saw in this plan a ruse to obtain names they did not wish to disclose and forbade more than one signature to appear on the receipt for all the goods delivered at a camp.

Elaborate formalities had to be completed before the delegates were allowed to enter the camps and internment centres. If they dared complain of the conditions they found in them they were warned that all Red Cross work would be stopped. Threatened with imprisonment and the confiscation of their property, they endured every conceivable form of insult and humiliation in their attempts to carry out the work they had undertaken. Altogether fourteen delegates lost their lives in the Far East; in North Borneo Doctor Vischer and his wife were flogged, tortured and shot because of their persistent attempts to help Allied prisoners of war.

It was only during the final months of the war that the Japanese government agreed to accept a new head for the Committee's delegation in Tokyo. They objected to the delegate travelling by the most straightforward route, via New York, San Francisco and Vladivostok, because it meant his passing through enemy territory; they eventually agreed to the journey which took him to Cairo, Teheran, Moscow, across Siberia to Manchukuo.

Doctor Junod had been selected for the post and finally reached Japan after the war in Europe had ended, and a week before the atomic bomb was dropped on Hiroshima.

8

'Charity in War'

The services to prisoners of war represented only a part of the great work of the Red Cross during and after the Second World War. The purpose for which it was originally founded—to render aid to sick and wounded in time of war—was never forgotten.

The British Red Cross Society and Order of St John of Jerusalem again joined forces, as they had in the First World War of 1914–18, and at one time or another their members served in all five continents.

The first V.A.D.s to be posted overseas left Britain for the Middle East before the war broke out, slipping away unnoticed by the public in August 1939. Thousands of men and women who had trained with the Red Cross in peacetime took their places in hospitals, ambulances, casualty stations, first aid posts and sick bays; the care of civilian victims of air raids became one of their major activities. During the Battle of Britain, members staffed first aid posts in London tubes and other shelters and all through the war shared in the work of the casualty services in cities, towns and villages.

Red Cross hospitals and convalescent homes were established, and supplies and comforts provided in immense quantities to meet the needs of the sick and wounded servicemen at home and abroad. As one of them wrote,

'Within half an hour of being wounded I was smoking

A stretcher-party in action after an air raid

Red Cross cigarettes. A few hours later I was in a pair of Red Cross pyjamas. I had my first shave for ten days, with a razor and blade, shaving brush, soap and mirror, also toothbrush and toothpaste, all supplied by the Red Cross. On the hospital ship, sweets and cigarettes were also supplied by the Red Cross. In the hospital I found that I was more comfortable if my stump was raised slightly, so I was given a small pillow and case—Red Cross. When I was fit to sit up, I used a Red Cross back-rest. I was taken to the cinema in a Red Cross wheel-chair—sometimes to a show arranged by the Red Cross. It seems that the capacity of the Red Cross and St John for doing good work is unlimited.'

The writer of the letter was one of many British sick and wounded men to benefit from a new service introduced in United Kingdom hospitals in 1942 and North Africa the following year.

Fighting had ended there in May 1943; but hospitals were full and Red Cross services needed for several months afterwards. Nurses were occupied with their regular duties and 'the boys', especially those who were convalescent, had nothing to do and no one to come and see them because there was no British community to undertake hospital visiting.

Life became pleasanter for them once the small pioneer party of Red Cross welfare officers arrived at the hospital. They arranged amusements and outings for the men who were well enough to enjoy them; they read to and wrote letters for those who were unable to read and write for themselves. They taught handicrafts to the bed-ridden and convalescent, gave out books and magazines and organized gramophone concerts. So greatly was their work appreciated by patients and hospital staff alike, that St John and Red Cross officers have continued their welfare work in every British Service hospital throughout the world.

Under the terms of the Geneva Convention for the sick and wounded, Red Cross societies of countries who have remained outside a conflict may send help, where they think fit, to the medical services or Red Cross society of a belligerent. Before the United States entered the war, the American Red Cross offered assistance to all national societies involved in hostilities and worked alongside the German and Polish societies for some time during the German occupation of Poland. American Red Cross funds were used to help Polish refugees in their scattered wanderings across Europe to Persia, East Africa and India; relief supplies and money for sick and wounded, sent to the Finnish Red Cross, ceased only when Finland was completely cut off by the fighting.

Had the Red Cross kept strictly to the terms of the Geneva Convention it would still have earned its great reputation. But the sentiments expressed in its motto, 'Charity in War', demanded more than that and impelled it to devise ways of helping people for whom no treaty existed. Its unceasing efforts to secure justice and mercy for them were amongst its finest endeavours during the Second World War.

The words *Inter Arma Caritas* (Charity in War) were first prefixed to a memoir on the International Committee of the Red Cross which was published on the twenty-fifth anniversary of its foundation. Gustave Moynier, the author of the words, had always hoped that they would in time be adopted as the motto of the Red Cross.

The word 'charity' has come to be associated almost exclusively with alms and almsgiving and has thereby lost much of its true meaning—love of one's neighbour—which the Red Cross restored to it during the Second World War.

Helping relatives who were separated by war to keep in touch with one another, and tracing and bringing together lost families, were two of the great charitable services of the Red Cross to millions of civilians in enemy hands; and those who turned to it in their distress found a living organization, which shared their anxieties and comforted them in their personal tragedies, and rejoiced with them when their news was good.

The feeling that someone was caring for their welfare and the bond of personal sympathy it created were so strong that to some people the Red Cross appeared to be a creature of flesh and blood, as was shown by one letter, addressed to 'Mrs Red Cross, Geneva', which read, 'My dear Geneva ... I happy to see that you think me always, and that you are interested in me. But on my side never forget you. I think often of you ...'.

The Red Cross Postal Message scheme, based on the Family News Service of the Spanish civil war, was a venture of the International Committee of the Red Cross, enabling civilians in enemy hands to keep in touch with their relatives when the normal postal services were completely severed between the countries at war. Forms were printed allowing space for a message of twenty-five words, which could be in English, French or German. When completed the messages were collected by the national societies, sent to the International Committee in Geneva where they were translated, and forwarded to the countries of destination. The replies followed a similar procedure. At first the messages could be exchanged only between families; later, they were extended to friends.

People from so many countries escaped and took refuge in the United Kingdom, or joined the fighting forces to continue the struggle from British shores, that the British Red Cross handled thousands of these messages. The scheme was practically world-wide; even places as remote as Ascension Island received and sent them. The International Committee and the national societies exchanged over twenty-five million of them during the war.

Proposals of marriage, news of the death of a member of the family or the arrival of a new baby, joys and sorrows great and small were imparted in the twenty-five words, relieving anxiety and bringing comfort to families divided by war. Even if the news was not always good, it was better than the absolute lack of it. 'You are the people that give us courage and confidence to keep going with these wonderful messages,' wrote one recipient; another, 'The liberation of my country gave me the opportunity to meet again my wife and parents with whom I had communicated during the last three years only through your care. I have to express my profound gratitude for your humanitarian services which I will remember during all my life.'

Often a message showed a pathetic struggle with the language in which it had been written, 'We are all in the love. I are old and I not pent in. My dauchter is not maried for I do not monies—Matus.' Sometimes the messages brought families closer simply through the homely way in which they were worded: one read, 'I can't write to you because my sister's baby is driving us mad', and another, 'I'm thinking of you whilst milking the cows'.

Messages for sailors spanned the world, taking months, even years to reach them. A Danish seaman, who had sailed from India in 1942 and left his ship at an Egyptian port, was handed news from his family two years later in Iceland. The first messages for sailors were sent to the crew of a small fighting trawler in July 1940; the last, for the men in the largest French battleship, the *Richelieu*, in 1945.

At times the Red Cross wondered if the censor, through whom every draft had to pass, would doubt the innocence of the cheerful greetings sent each month by a young French airman to his seven little brothers and sisters, especially as the children all had funny nicknames which could have been taken for code words; or would suspect the sentiments of the man who wrote regularly to his sweetheart of 'cliffs, waves and seagulls', until all doubts were dispelled by the arrival of a wedding invitation in 1944. The censor did object, however, to the message from a girl who announced to her parents, 'I have become engaged. My fiancé is tall and dark and has wings', and returned it heavily blue-pencilled for redrafting.

Many of the messages developed into inquiries about relatives from whom no reply had been received. All too often the envelope was returned, marked, 'Deported to an unknown destination'.

When German forces began sweeping across Europe and occupying it, families were separated and scattered all over the world. The Red Cross received a flood of inquiries for and from people who were missing from their homes, or anxious about the relatives they had left behind after they themselves had escaped from a country. The Tracing Files of the Red Cross, with their records of lost relatives found and restored to their loved ones, contain some of the most dramatic stories of the war and would provide an author with the plot for a book far beyond any that could be imagined. As the war continued and greater numbers of civilians were caught up in it, the Tracing service grew until there were few countries to which it was not extended. But the inquiries reached their peak when hostilities ended; the search for lost relatives continued for many years and unhappily continues to this day.

People placed a touching faith in the powers of the Red Cross. 'Please trace Mr ——, a Latvian, aged seventy-five,' was one request made to the British Red Cross. 'If he is above ground I know that you will find him.'

Many of the inquiries the society received were from Frenchmen caught up in the changing fortunes of their country. One French family with connexions numbered no fewer than four hundred and forty-nine members, each of whom wanted to be put in touch with the others.

How Moses found a brother when he thought all his family were dead was one of numerous chance inquiries that ended in bringing people together. Moses was a Czechoslovakian boy who had been brought to England where, for some years, he had been living in a refugee hostel. A faint hope that one of his brothers who served in the Czech army might be alive prompted him to ask the Red Cross to start inquiries. Some time afterwards, the Red Cross received a tracing inquiry from a Czech of the same name, living in the United Kingdom and trying to find a brother in the Czech army. The Red Cross telephoned him and asked if by chance he had a brother called 'Moses'. The man was terribly distressed; he once had a little brother of that name, he said, but he had been killed with the rest of his family in Czechoslovakia. After again examining the records of the case, the Red Cross broke the good news to him that Moses was not only alive but had been inquiring after him. The two brothers were happily re-united in England, where they had been living for two or three years believing each other dead.

Another inquiry concerned a dog and was from the mother of an airman who had been killed. Her son had been devoted to 'Gyp' and often mentioned him in his letters. She wanted to know where the dog was and who was caring for it. Gyp was traced by the Red Cross and a photograph of him with his new master was sent to the airman's mother, with the assurance that he had a good home and was being well looked after.

With the help of the British Red Cross Josef and Klara's problems were happily resolved, but while they were being disentangled the society became deeply involved in the young couple's affairs, exchanging their messages and even being asked to give advice. Klara lived in Dusseldorf; Josef in Szeged, Hungary, and described himself as 'a paint artist now learning the jure at the university'.

A soldier in the Hungarian forces, he had met Klara in a Red Cross hospital in Germany. Later he was taken prisoner by the Americans who afterwards repatriated him. He received many letters from Klara but was unable to send any to her in Germany.

'Klara comme soon. Wait no more. In this year we shall to live in America. I have pappers for you also too', Josef wrote, and was delighted when he heard that the Red Cross had sent the message, 'because I had look my matter hopeless. Through America, Swiss and Hungarian Red Cross, through Holland, Luxembourg and Austria I had try to send letters to my wife, but she don't received nothing'. Klara's reply, equally delighted, asked him for a photograph of himself and a pen and ink sketch of a merry-looking young man was forwarded to her.

But a little later Josef wrote to tell the Red Cross, 'We have a grand sorrow with my wife. She is waiting for my, and I am also waiting for her. She me writes that I must comme to Germany. What are you think? What is best?' As he had work, the Red Cross advised him to stay where he was and wait for Klara to join him in course of time. It was impossible for him to do anything else just then, as he was in Eastern Hungary and she in Western Germany. Josef took the advice, but shortly afterwards wrote to say he would be waiting for Klara in Austria from 6th to 10th December, and begged the Red Cross to send her a 'telegramme'. Klara replied, 'I'm to start on January 3rd and try the way without other help', though this was in the middle of a very cold winter.

Klara and Josef were eventually reunited; but not before many adventures had befallen Klara and frantic letters had reached the Red Cross from Josef. Klara arrived after a forty-day journey, during which she had spent three weeks in Salzburg and a week in prison at Sopron because, as Josef explained, 'She don't haddet pappers to leave countreys. Now she is alright at home'.

They both wrote charming letters of thanks to the Red Cross; though when their file was finally closed the course of true love was still not running quite smoothly. Poor Josef wrote to say he 'had the Muns (mumps) and not just this, others have I too'.

Throughout the last few months of the war before Germany's 'unconditional surrender', the Allied advance and air attacks on German railways and marshalling yards seriously dislocated the transport of supplies to the prisoner of war camps. Matters became even more serious when the German authorities ordered the camps on the Eastern front to be moved nearer the centre of Germany.

In the bitterly cold weather of February 1945, and with no more than an hour or two's warning in which to prepare themselves, British, American and Allied prisoners were ordered out of the camps and set on long forced-marches with scarcely any food.

This brought about one of the most dramatic services for prisoners of war yet thought of by the Red Cross. There was nothing in the Geneva Conventions to say how such a situation should be met; but the International Committee succeeded in obtaining from the harassed German administration a plan of the routes the prisoners were following and formal permission to try and reach them. Convoys of trucks, painted white, each one marked on the roof and sides with a huge red cross, set off from Geneva loaded with food and other supplies. Fanning out and threading their way through the chaos and military confusion on the roads, they searched out the columns of weary prisoners in by-ways and country lanes, where they came upon them marching or resting by the roadside. The trucks also met with former concentration camp victims who were now fugitives on the roads, and gave out food, medical supplies and warm clothing to them, leaving with them quantities of hay and firewood, until the vehicles could return to pick them up and take them to safety.

Several Canadian prisoners of war volunteered for the task of driving the trucks; and although at Constance there was no more than a barrier between them and freedom in Switzerland, none took advantage of the chance to escape.

The prisoners called the trucks 'The White Ladies'; and along with his memories of the Red Cross parcels service, no prisoner of war will ever forget his joy and gratitude when the convoys hove in sight and found him.

The White Ladies criss-crossed over hundreds of miles of German roads, seeking out the prisoners and showing them to the last that the Red Cross had not forgotten them.

By a strange coincidence V.E. (Victory in Europe) Day was the one hundred and seventeenth anniversary of the birth of Henri Dunant—the man who had felt the cause of prisoners of war so deeply and devoted so much of his life to securing better conditions for them.

9
The Years that Followed

On part of a ruined building left standing in four square miles of rubble, all that remained of the seventh largest city in Japan, the hands of a clock had stopped at a quarter past eight. It marked the time of Hiroshima's destruction on 6th August 1945 and the birth of the Atomic Age.

This horrifying event, and the second nuclear bomb dropped three days later on Nagasaki, nevertheless brought to an end the sufferings of countless men, women and children in Japanese hands. The news that the war was over spread from camp to camp and was borne out in the skies when hundreds of coloured parachutes, opening out like flowers, dropped parcels of food into the captives' midst.

Soon, all those who were well enough to travel were going home. British prisoners and interned civilians returned through the Red Sea and Mediterranean or across the Pacific, United States and Atlantic. The sea voyage did them an immense amount of good, helping to build up their health and strength. British Red Cross welfare officers accompanied them and welcomed them with clothing and comforts at the ports, and distributed among them copies of a specially prepared newspaper, *News from Britain*, recording the major events that had taken place during the years the captives had been without news of home.

After helping with the initial stages of their release, Doctor Junod and the other delegates of the International Committee went to Hiroshima. A telegram from one of the delegates already there appealed for drugs, medical supplies and blood plasma for the emergency hospitals set up by the Japanese, and a rescue operation was at once organized.

Meanwhile among the ruins of Europe the Red Cross was shouldering the immense task of relieving the suffering and distress left behind by the war.

Teams of British Red Cross workers, following on the heels of the victorious Allied armies, had started relief work for thousands of displaced Poles from Soviet Russia, and refugees from Greece and other Balkan countries who had fled to Egypt in 1942. Relief teams entered Italy at the beginning of 1944, Austria a year later.

As the Allied armies moved forward from the Normandy beaches and the countries were liberated, the relief teams began work in France, Belgium, Holland and Luxembourg. Finally, they entered Germany itself. The most distressing task they carried out about this time was in the notorious Belsen concentration camp, where seventy-five British Red Cross members arrived shortly after it had been uncovered and helped to look after the sixty thousand inmates.

The Red Cross societies of Holland and Belgium were soon able to take over their own relief work; but in Germany the scale of misery and want was unparalleled. Close on a million and a half displaced persons, men, women and children of many nationalities, victims of the concentration camps and slave workers of the German forced-labour systems, had been torn from their homes in countries hundreds of miles away. Most of them were in

desperate need of medical attention and became the
immediate care of the relief teams. The military authorities opened camps and took over former German barracks, which were so vast that several thousand people
were housed in them. Entering one of these camps gave

the impression of arriving at a small town with its own hospital, clinics and dental surgeries, workshops, barber's shop, stores, printing works, garage and vehicle-repair shops, its own church, school and wireless station broadcasting programmes throughout the camp. By being usefully occupied the inmates were encouraged to pick up the broken threads of their lives.

In time some of them were repatriated; others, unwilling or unable to return to their own countries, were offered the chance to emigrate and start life afresh in Commonwealth countries or South America. But before these countries would accept them, the displaced persons had to attain a certain standard of physical fitness. Sometimes a family group was held back by a delicate child or an elderly relative, and the British Red Cross took the faltering members under its wing, giving them extra food and vitamins to build up their health.

Before long it became clear that the German people needed helping as much as the displaced persons. The German Red Cross, disorganized and depleted, was unable to take over their welfare.

When Germany surrendered the country was divided into four zones occupied by American, British, French and Soviet armies. The British zone had suffered extensive damage and thousands of people, their homes destroyed, were living in overcrowded conditions in former air raid shelters and the cellars of bombed-out houses. The army authorities realized that something must be done for them if famine and epidemics were to be averted. The British Red Cross was asked to carry

isplaced Persons in 1945; two or more
milies often lived in one room

out relief services for the German people as well as for displaced persons.

In many of the larger cities such as Hamburg and Berlin the Germans had put up immense, fortress-like buildings, constructed from materials which were virtually indestructible. They were called 'bunkers' and highly effective they proved to be. These mammoth reminders of the former Nazi regime now became the refuge of scores of German families, who lived in the warren of chambers deep underground. The 'bunker population', as these people were called, was easily recognizable by their sullen expressions and the grey skins they acquired from being deprived of fresh air and light.

Day after day hordes of German refugees, believing that freedom for them lay just on the other side of the frontier, crossed from the East to swell the ranks of homeless people in the already overcrowded towns and cities of the West. In time these unfortunate wanderers were housed in some of the camps and barracks vacated by the displaced persons.

The relief teams organized communal feeding schemes for them and opened orphanages, kindergartens and holiday camps for the children. Hospitals and sunlight clinics were set up, and six sanatoria, equipped by various Red Cross societies, for the treatment of tuberculosis which was widespread.

Among the schemes organized for the German children were 'Operation Waif' for the war orphans of Berlin, fifty of whom were taken each week to a children's home, where they stayed in quarantine for three weeks before being sent to foster-parents, and 'Operation Shamrock,' under which the Irish Red Cross invited parties of children to stay with families in Ireland until

At the beginning of 1946 it was estimated that there were 1,675,000 refugees

conditions improved in Germany. The German welfare societies selected the children; the British Red Cross provided the escorts for their journeys and arranged their overnight accommodation in Britain on the way through.

Finally there was the work carried out by the Red Cross for the German prisoners of war released from the camps in Russia. The point of arrival for these prisoners was a small strip of no man's land where the British,

American and Russian zones met. Marked by a wooden beam across the road and guarded by a single Russian sentry, it was called Friedland. The prisoners came through the frontier post at irregular intervals, sometimes in hundreds, at others mere handfuls; occasionally women and children were among them. Hungry, dirty and ragged, most of them were weak and ill. It is a Red Cross tradition to help prisoners without regard to the side on which they have fought, and the German and British Red Cross societies worked hard to bring some comfort to these hopeless, broken people.

In the three western zones of Germany and Austria the British Red Cross also looked after needy British and British-born people, many of them women who, before and after the First World War, had married Germans or gone as nannies and governesses to German families and who were now living on diminished pensions on the family estates. Food parcels and clothing were distributed to them, and welfare centres resembling clubs were formed in the larger towns, where they could meet other British-born people, borrow books and do handicrafts. Some of them learnt first aid and undertook hospital visiting.

The centre for German limbless ex-servicemen, established by the British Red Cross at Bad Pyrmont, once a fashionable spa on the borders of Hanover, was modelled on the world famous centre at Roehampton and came as an innovation in Germany, where nothing like it had hitherto existed. Rehabilitation of the limbless, which had been developed with such success in Britain during the war, was unknown to the Germans at this time, and brought new hope to thousands of disabled men. Many of them had fought on the Russian front, where limb amputations were sadly frequent, owing to the aggravation of wounds by frostbite and the long delays in getting to hospitals. At Bad Pyrmont these men were given the most up-to-date treatment, were fitted with artificial limbs made at the centre's workshops and, most important of all, trained to earn a livelihood. The centre was directed by a handful of experts, part of whose task was to teach the Germans the work so that they could continue it after the British Red Cross withdrew.

Although the Red Cross teams saw concentration camps and other signs of former German brutality, they carried out their tasks for these suffering people without prejudice; helping those who, but a short while before, had sought to destroy them, and showing them the same compassion which had moved Dunant and the women of Castiglione to recognize that 'All men are brothers'. A German woman, who had received no help from the British Red Cross, paid tribute to their impartiality in a letter, in which she wrote, 'In 1945 your armies conquered our country, but afterwards your Red Cross conquered our hearts'.

The end of the war gave members of the Junior Red Cross many opportunities of fulfilling its aim to foster 'international friendship and understanding'. In some countries the Red Cross societies had been hard at work throughout the war and had built up large resources from their wartime appeals; in others, the societies were virtually non-existent, or lacked funds and an organization of any strength. Junior sections of one country sent supplies and equipment to help the junior sections of another to restart their work.

Everywhere there were children who had suffered in the war and gifts of food, clothing, medicines, vitamins and toys from the junior sections helped to bring comfort and better health to countless numbers of them. American juniors equipped fifty sewing-rooms for girls and fifty workshops for boys in refugee camps in Germany; Irish Juniors adopted schools there and in Austria and Italy; Canadian juniors sent cocoa and orange juice to help the Czechoslovak Red Cross with its supplementary feeding schemes for children, and British juniors sent canteens of knives and forks to Yugoslav juniors who were short of them for the school-feeding scheme they were carrying out.

One of the first acts of the Luxembourg Junior Red Cross, formed after the war, was to send fifteen tons of toys and sweets to children in refugee and displaced persons' camps. In the Grand Duchy, 5th December is the day when St Nicholas takes round a donkey loaded with sweets and toys to put on the plates which the children leave ready outside their doors. Each child contributed something from his plate towards the gift that was finally collected and sent to the camps.

These are but a few examples of the ways in which young people helped young people, many of whom had never known anything but war and distress in their short lives.

Before the British Red Cross teams had been withdrawn from Germany, the society had recruited other teams for a relief operation in Jordan.

In May 1948 Israel was proclaimed an independent State and a fierce war broke out between Israel and the Arab States. By September a large-scale refugee problem had arisen; over nine hundred thousand were destitute and the United Nations asked the Red Cross to plan and carry out a relief programme for them. The International

Committee operated in the areas still affected by the war, where the presence of a neutral intermediary was imperative; the League of Red Cross Societies recruited an international team of doctors, nurses, emergency relief specialists and administrative experts from nineteen national societies and undertook the operations in Lebanon and Syria; the British Red Cross assumed responsibility for the entire medical programme in Jordan and helped with the formation of the national Red Crescent Society.

The relief operation, planned to last nine months, was extended to sixteen; and it was the largest the League had undertaken in the thirty years of its existence. Once the danger of starvation was over, a social welfare programme was carried out for the refugees; camp schools were opened and sewing centres, shoe-making and soap-making projects were started. The Red Cross eventually handed over to the United Nations Relief and Works Agency for Palestine Refugees created for this purpose; but a number of national societies continued to send relief supplies, especially clothing.

An important event in the history of the Red Cross and, indeed, of civilization, took place on 12th August 1949. The diplomatic representatives of fifty-nine States, assembled in Geneva, revised the texts of the former Geneva Conventions and approved a new Convention for the protection of civilians in wartime.

The idea of such a Convention had been put forward by the Red Cross some years before the Second World War; unfortunately, war was declared before the diplomatic conference which was to study the proposals could meet.

World opinion had been profoundly shocked by the

inhuman treatment of countless civilians in the war and when it ended the Red Cross, with all the fresh evidence it had collected, drafted and submitted to governments a Convention to prevent a repetition of such suffering.

That the Red Cross, which is not a governmental institution and has no authority to speak for governments, should be concerned in the making of these international treaties is one of its most remarkable features.

The explanation is a historical one: the first Geneva Convention of 1864 was inspired by the Committee of Five (the forerunner of the International Committee of the Red Cross) and the preparation of subsequent Conventions has become the Committee's traditional function.

Signing a convention at a conference does not mean that a country is then bound by its terms; it must afterwards be formally and officially ratified by the government of the country.

It is difficult for later generations to appreciate the immense importance of these humanitarian conventions, which have won a right of way for mercy in the midst of bitter hostility. Quite apart from outlawing much of the cruelty which was practised in former times, they have made a breach in the usages of war, allowing defenceless victims to be placed under the protection of prohibitive laws. Such conventions have sometimes even been invoked to place a check on violence in conflicts where neither party has signed or ratified them.

10

Korea

It is not generally realized that there was a Korean Red Cross in Henri Dunant's lifetime. The society was established by Imperial Decree in October 1905, five years before Dunant's death and rather more than a month after the Treaty of Portsmouth was signed by the belligerents at the end of the Russo-Japanese war.

Both the war and the Treaty were to affect the destiny of Korea and its newly-formed Red Cross society in an unpredictable way four years later.

Ninety years before, after a short victorious war against China (with Korea as one of its main issues), Japan had made China declare Korea's independence and had respected it herself. But after she emerged victorious from the Russo-Japanese war, which had been fought mainly to decide which of the two powers should possess Korea, Japan annexed the country under the terms of the Treaty of Portsmouth.

Korea was re-named and known as Chosen (Land of Morning Calm) for the next thirty-five years; her Red Cross society became a branch of the Japanese Red Cross.

Although the society lost its independence several fine Red Cross hospitals and clinics were built in the country during this period, and its membership at the time of the Second World War was estimated at four and a half million.

Early in the war the Allies promised Korea her independence. But when Japan was conquered in 1945 Korea was divided at the 38th Parallel, Russia taking the surrender of Japanese forces in the north, the United States that of the forces in the south. Thus North and South Korea were brought into being as two separate countries.

The North Korean Red Cross Society was recognized by the government of the Democratic People's Republic of Korea and its work included operating some thousands of health service stations and health protection units.

In South Korea the Red Cross society made a promising new start in 1947, modernizing its hospitals and clinics with the help of the American Red Cross and developing an active programme of medical care and health education for the people. Unfortunately, misfortune was all too soon to overtake this ill-fated national society, whose efforts were directed towards helping a people who stood so much in need of them.

On 25th June 1950 South Korea was invaded by the armed forces of Communist North Korea. The United Nations called upon its members to go to the help of South Korea and United States forces landed shortly afterwards. By the beginning of September British and Commonwealth troops were also in action. The North Koreans were driven back; but in November Chinese forces entered the conflict and for over two and a half years Korea was the scene of bitter fighting.

The South Korean Red Cross (later to be known as the Republic of Korea Red Cross) was driven from its headquarters in Seoul, the capital, but, reassembling at Taegu and Pusan, began relief work for hundreds of refugees, treating patients at dispensaries and clinics and tending wounded Korean soldiers.

Early in February the following year Red Cross medical welfare teams, sent at the request of the League of Red Cross Societies, arrived in Korea from Britain, Canada, Denmark and Norway to undertake relief work among the civilian population and the large number of refugees who were seeking food, protection and shelter in the small zone remaining under United Nations control. Red Cross and Red Crescent societies of over sixteen countries sent help in the form of medical supplies and clothing to relieve the sufferings of these helpless people, many of whom did not know what the war was about.

The International Committee of the Red Cross supplied medical aid for the war victims of both North and South Korea. The Chinese Red Cross sent seven medical teams, and food, clothing, medicines, surgical instruments and other forms of relief for the civilian population of North Korea; the Bulgarian Red Cross contributed a sanitary team, and the Red Cross societies of Hungary, Poland, Romania and Soviet Russia staffed field hospitals.

The national societies of the countries involved in the fighting provided their traditional services for the sick and wounded of their forces. British Red Cross Naval V.A.D.s served in H.M. Hospital ship *Maine* which evacuated British and Commonwealth wounded from South Korea to hospitals in Japan, where they were looked after by Commonwealth Red Cross Hospital Visitors and St John and Red Cross Service Hospitals Welfare Officers, who carried out the duties for which they had become so well-known in the Second World War.

In September 1950, the Swedish Red Cross established in Pusan a field hospital for civilian and Service wounded and sick. The following March, the Danish Red Cross fitted out a hospital ship, the *Jutlandia*, for duty in Korean waters. The ship made three voyages from Japan to Europe during the war, repatriating seven hundred patients and one hundred and sixty-five prisoners to Belgium, Ethiopia, France, Greece, the Netherlands, Turkey and Britain. The Danish society sent a field unit, which operated at the front line, and the Italian Red Cross a hospital mission.

After the armistice was signed on 27th July 1953, teams composed of Red Cross representatives from North Korea, China and the countries which had contributed forces to the United Nations, took part in 'Operation Big Switch' at Panmunjom, providing the doctors, nurses and social workers for ninety-five thousand prisoners of war who were repatriated. Over twenty-three thousand, who refused repatriation, were held in the neutral zone of Korea and looked after by the Indian Red Cross.

Once again the war-stricken population was in desperate need. In South Korea the Red Cross was deprived of even the most elementary means of restarting its work. All the clinics and dispensaries were in ruins. The hospital and nursing school in Seoul had been severely damaged and nothing remained of the interior furnishings or valuable medical equipment; the tuberculosis sanatorium at the seaside resort of Inchon had suffered similarly.

Gifts of money to help rebuild these Red Cross establishments came from national societies all over the world.

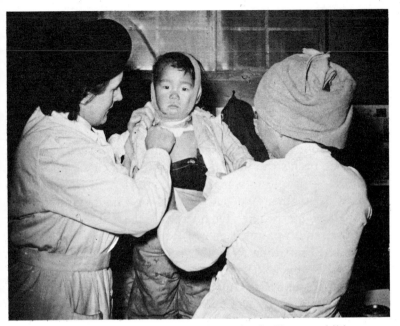

Sister Ella Jorden dressing the neck of a Korean child

'We could do with a ton of rags!' a British Red Cross nurse wrote in her first report from Korea. She and another trained nurse had been sent by the society to help the South Korean Red Cross with its relief work for civilians and arrived in Seoul a month or two after the armistice.

In the hospital they found the patients lying on the bare springs of the beds, and there was not enough linen for each of them to have a sheet. The nurses could find neither towels, bowls, cloths nor water with which to wash the sick. Lack of water was in fact one of the worst problems in war-devastated Seoul; it was rationed and ran for about an hour a day. The patients were surrounded by their relatives, who made charcoal fires in the wards to cook what little food they had managed to buy. At night the beds were usually shared, for the relatives and friends had no homes to return to, and the cold was intense. Conditions were scarcely better in the sanatorium at Inchon, where only one floor of the building was usable and forty-eight very sick children were housed.

But Sister Ella Jorden, who had sighed for the rags, was not discouraged by the task confronting her. Much of her life had been spent in bringing order out of chaos among suffering people in war-scarred countries. In her early days as a nurse she had worked in China, until the Japanese interned her. On her release she had walked out of the camp wearing a pair of Red Cross shoes and had remained in China to work with the British Red Cross for the people who were too sick to be repatriated. Soon after her return to England, the society sent her to Germany, where she nursed the displaced persons, refugees and the 'bunker population'. Later she was sent with the British Red Cross commission to Jordan, and organized a hospital for Arab refugees. She then worked for the Red Cross in Malaya, taking a mobile dispensary into the jungle and treating many sick people in primitive conditions.

In a remarkably short time she and her colleague brought the hospital at Seoul and the sanatorium at Inchon into working order. The wards were scrubbed and re-equipped; surplus invalid food parcels, no longer needed for prisoners of war, were sent from Kure and provided diets for the patients. Forty young Korean girls began their training at the nursing school under the tuition of the nurses, who also operated a mobile dispensary, equipped and presented by the British Red Cross, for the sick who were unable to get into the city.

Before long, in response to a special appeal to Red

Cross branches all over the United Kingdom, hundreds of parcels began arriving in Seoul. There were four different kinds of parcel; containing clothes and linen for adults, children, toddlers and babies. The contents of each parcel were indicated by the code on the label, saving the nurses hours of sorting and unpacking when the packages were opened at the hospital. Imagination as well as forethought went into planning what should go into them. Among the sleeping-suits, socks, cot-sheets and other items in the parcels for toddlers and babies the Red Cross did not forget to enclose '*one soft toy*'.

Two welfare officers joined the nurses the following spring and for many months carried out an immense amount of work among the homeless people in and around Seoul.

Sister Ella Jorden's story has been told in newspaper and magazine articles, on the wireless and in a book, entitled *Operation Mercy*. She was made a Member of the British Empire in the New Year Honours of 1954 and the following year received the Florence Nightingale Medal, the highest award that can be bestowed upon a Red Cross nurse and given to those who best exemplify its ideal.

The idea for this Medal was first proposed by a representative of the Hungarian Red Cross in 1912; since when it has been presented by the International Committee of the Red Cross every two years and many brave nurses are numbered among its recipients.

11

The Red Cross and the Refugees

'What kind of people can live in houses?'

The child who asked this question belonged to the legion of human beings who down the ages have been uprooted by war, persecution and political change, to swell the ranks of the dispersed and dispossessed known as refugees.

He and his parents were among thousands of families who lived in refugee camps following the Second World War. Later they joined the millions of people, now happily resettled throughout the world, who at one time were refugees and were helped to a new life by the Red Cross.

Had they been refugees about forty years earlier they would also have known and revered the name of the great Norwegian, Doctor Fridtjof Nansen, who as a result of the initiative taken by the Red Cross in 1921 was appointed the first High Commissioner for Refugees.

The refugee problem, which had reached alarming proportions at the time of Nansen's appointment, began in 1913 when the first groups of Bulgarians, of whom over two hundred thousand had been deported to neighbouring countries, returned to their native land and were re-established by the Red Cross. From 1915 onwards the Red Cross and various private charities also helped large numbers of Armenians in Asia Minor and refugees of other nationalities in different European countries. But in 1918 and the three following years, when a million and a half people left Russia to escape the effects of famine and political upheavals, the Red Cross and other associations which were helping the refugees realized that the remedy for their plight was beyond the power of purely humanitarian organizations.

On 16th February 1921, the International Committee of the Red Cross called a meeting of the associations (among which was the League of Red Cross Societies) who were engaged in relief for Russian refugees. It was decided to lay the problem before the League of Nations and suggest the appointment of a Commissioner to co-ordinate their work. The letter supporting the proposal expressed the International Committee's gratitude to Nansen, who had just completed the immense task of repatriating four hundred thousand prisoners of war, and no doubt influenced the League of Nations' decision to nominate him to the post of High Commissioner for Refugees.

Nansen was already famous as an Arctic explorer, a natural historian, botanist, professor of zoology and oceanography, a diplomatist (he had furthered the separation of Norway and Sweden in 1905 and been Norwegian minister in London from 1906–8) and as the author of several books. The story of his adventurous journey across Greenland had stirred the world, as had his ingenious attempt to reach the North Pole, when his specially built ship, the *Fram*, was deliberately trapped in the pack ice; they drifted northward with the current until, finally, he and Johansen pushed across the ice to the furthest point north till then attained by man.

As High Commissioner for Refugees, Nansen applied himself with equal energy to solving the Russian refugee problem for which, in 1922, eight years before his death, he was awarded the Nobel Peace Prize; and in the execution of his plans he laid the foundations of all future international refugee relief work.

On his appointment he at once called upon the International Committee of the Red Cross to help him. The close co-operation they then established has continued between the Red Cross and succeeding intergovernmental refugee agencies.

The Red Cross was already aiding refugees of Spanish and other nationalities in France when the Second World War broke out. Its relief activities, on behalf of the civilian populations of occupied countries during the war and after they were liberated, included help for the refugees who were living in them. In subsequent years Red Cross aid was given to over thirty-five million people uprooted from their homes in Eastern Europe, India, Palestine, China, Korea and Vietnam.

The upheavals in these countries occurred prior to 1956, when the Hungarian Uprising created a refugee situation almost without precedent in volume and suddenness. The extensive relief measures undertaken by the International Committee of the Red Cross in Budapest and other parts of Hungary, by the League of Red Cross Societies and its member societies in Austria, Yugoslavia, the countries through which the refugees passed and those in which they were resettled, are now entered in the pages of history.

The news on 23rd October that fighting had broken out in Budapest shocked no one more than the League of Red Cross Societies' staff who, less than a month before, had completed in Hungary the final distributions of food to the hundred thousand victims of the Danube floods in the spring. Anxiety increased when the Hungarian Red Cross Society's broadcast appeal for medical supplies ended abruptly and all attempts failed to establish communication with the society. While the League continued its efforts to obtain more precise details of the Hungarian society's needs, offers of help and requests for information poured in from other national societies, who had heard the broadcast and were standing by ready to send supplies and personnel. Six hours later, when the Hungarian Red Cross telephoned Geneva, help was on its way.

A brief lull in the fighting ended soon after the Red Cross teams reached Budapest; they were obliged to withdraw and the Hungarian frontiers were closed. Only delegates of the International Committee, who had flown in with initial supplies of blood plasma and medicines, were accepted. The delegates remained in Hungary eight months, attending to the wounded in the streets of Budapest, and when the frontiers reopened to admit relief distributing about thirty thousand tons of food, medicines, clothing and household goods (including nine thousand tons of coal contributed by the Red Cross and governments) to over a million Hungarians, who without this help would undoubtedly have died of cold and starvation.

Meanwhile, the large consignments of relief goods pouring in from all parts of the world and piling up in depots in Vienna were destined to be used for a new situation which was developing along Austria's Burgenland frontier with Hungary. A mass exodus of Hungarians had begun, at first at the rate of about a thousand a

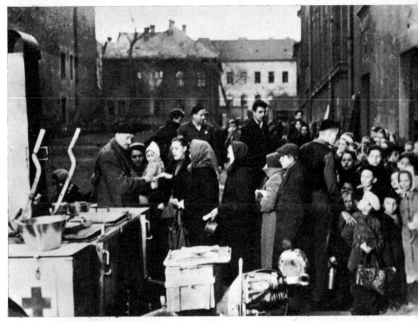

Budapest, the Hungarian Uprising of 1956. The delegates of the International Committee were able to supply the people with food, milk, blankets and window-panes

week and, by the end of November, six thousand a day; many of them in family groups. The majority of the refugees were young and able-bodied; elderly or sick would not have survived the long walk, especially in its final stages where the land was marshy and had to be crossed in the bitterly cold weather under cover of darkness.

The large influx of refugees placed a considerable strain on the economy of Austria, which was not only a smaller country than Hungary but already was giving shelter to about a hundred and fourteen thousand war-time refugees and displaced persons under United Nations mandate; and so acute was the housing shortage in the country that many Austrians were living in camps and barracks.

The turn of events opened up a fresh relief operation centred on Vienna. While the League recruited helpers from its member societies and assumed responsibility for the reception, care and shelter of the Hungarian refugees, the United Nations High Commissioner appealed to governments to grant asylum to as many of them as possible.

The prompt response to his request set in motion the large-scale emigration of refugees which figured so prominently in this relief undertaking. In the next ten weeks the Red Cross, in co-operation with the United

A camp for Hungarian refugees in Austria

Nations High Commissioner and the Inter-governmental Committee for European Migration, moved a hundred thousand people by land, sea and air to over twenty-eight countries. The national societies looked after the refugees on the journeys which took some of them across the world to Iceland, Australia and New Zealand, North and South America, met them on arrival in these countries and helped with their resettlement.

In Austria barracks, orphanages, hospitals, hotels, castles, groups of wooden huts and even a restaurant were hastily converted into refugee camps; fifty-two societies sending helpers to work in them. To provide the refugees with occupation and leisure activities, they were supplied with sets of tools, games and sports equipment, sewing-machines, cloth and the materials for needlework and embroidery. Classes were arranged for the adults to learn driving, engineering, typing, dress-making, photography and languages. The national Junior sections responded generously to the League's appeals for the children, and in addition to sending them toys, games, radiograms and other recreational supplies, raised sufficient money to pay for each child to be fitted out with a warm new outfit. In time nurseries and kindergartens were opened for the children, some of whom went to the local schools.

Since early November some hundreds of refugees had been heading south and entering Yugoslavia (which is nearly three times the size of Hungary) and thousands crossed into the country from late December onwards when the Austrian frontier was more effectively sealed. The relief operation in Yugoslavia was similar to that carried out in Austria, though no helpers from other national societies were needed. The Yugoslav Red Cross was supplied with food, clothing, bedding, medicines and other items from the reserves in Vienna, and additional contributions from several of the national societies equipped entire camps. Bela Crkva, near the Romanian frontier, a camp housing over four hundred refugee children under eighteen who had fled without their parents, received many gifts from national Junior sections. The camp, under a leader and Red Cross welfare worker, was run entirely by the children themselves and became a model of good care and organization.

The Hungarian operation, originally planned for thirty days, lasted eleven months. In September 1957 the League of Red Cross Societies was awarded the Nansen Medal, which is presented each year for outstanding services to refugees. It was the first time that it had been conferred upon an organization rather than an individual and honoured the many national societies who had 'contributed so much, so quickly'.

Before the relief operation had ended in Hungary another vast refugee situation had begun to develop in North Africa.

Since 1954, when armed conflict broke out in Algeria, large numbers of the population which inhabited the territories bordering on Morocco and Tunisia had been seeking asylum in these two countries. Three years later fifty thousand Algerian refugees were in Tunisia, forty thousand in Morocco; their numbers doubling a year afterwards and continuing to increase as time passed.

The solution to the problem was simple enough to the refugees: when the fighting ended they would go home. But the Red Cross, which had already given them some assistance, viewed matters rather differently. Since its relief operation in conjunction with the United Nations

High Commissioner began in February 1959, the refugees' condition, especially that of the children, had deteriorated alarmingly; and they required help on a substantial scale if any of them in the uncertain future was to return to Algeria.

Deprived of their breadwinners the refugees, most of whom were women, children and old people, were penniless and in need of food, clothing to replace their rags, and tents or other shelter than the mountain caves they were inhabiting, and the *gourbis* they had put together from mud and branches which gave them little protection against the bitter cold of the winter nights, snowstorms and rain.

Medical care for an Algerian refugee; eye disorders were prevalent

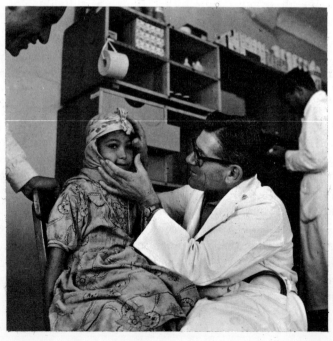

Algerian refugee children with some of the supplies given to
them by the Red Cross

For the next three years the refugees were supplied
with monthly rations of wheat, sugar, oil, pulses and
soap from sixty-two distribution centres in their countries of exile; and received medical attention at the
dispensaries organized for them by French-speaking
nurses from the national societies. Every day a hundred
thousand children were given each a slice of bread and a
cup of warm milk (the gift of the national Junior sections,
who contributed one million three hundred thousand
tins of milk); and twelve thousand children attending at
the tented schools which had been installed for them in

the remote, mountainous *Bec de Canard* (Duck's Beak) region of Tunisia, received bowls of soup. Centres equipped with looms and sewing-machines were opened for the women and materials provided for them to make their native dress and weave alfalfa mats. Before each winter set in warm clothing and blankets were distributed to them and their tents were replaced.

With the declaration of the Evian Cease-fire agreements in March 1962 the Red Cross organized the repatriation of these Algerian people. Departure centres manned by Red Cross medical teams were established at various points along the frontiers; as the refugees, in parties of from six to twelve hundred, arrived at them they were vaccinated for smallpox and issued with passports, and each refugee received a month's supply of rations so that none should arrive home without food.

The repatriation took two months to complete. When the teams finished their work at the departure centres they joined those of the French Red Cross, who had started in Algeria an extensive resettlement scheme for the refugees, many of whom had returned to find their homes and villages in ruins. The programme also included emergency relief for the Algerian population; the children especially had suffered acutely during the fighting and were by now in such desperate need that it was feared unless something were immediately done for them few would survive the coming winter.

It is not often that a refugee problem has ended as happily as this one, with the return to their native land in 1962 of some one hundred and twenty thousand people; several of whom had been exiles for nearly eight years.

Emergency relief for the Algerians in Morocco and

A floating dispensary in Vietnam, capable of transporting six people, or four with medical supplies and a folding stretcher

Tunisia came first from the International Committee of the Red Cross, as neither Red Crescent society in the countries of asylum had been established. On numerous other occasions when a large-scale refugee exodus has suddenly taken place in a country, the Red Cross has already been there and acted before intergovernmental relief has been started.

During the conflict in Laos between 1961 and 1963, large sections of the population became 'national refugees', abandoning their homes and fleeing to other parts of the country as the fighting spread, arriving on foot, by canoe, helicopter and plane, all with one thing in common—their urgent need of relief. The Committee's delegates, as well as carrying out their traditional duties in a country at war, distributed foodstuffs and clothing, provided by the national societies, to some twelve thousand displaced people.

The plight of thousands of bewildered and destitute national refugees in war-ravaged Vietnam led to relief operations being undertaken for them by the League of Red Cross Societies. In addition to sending vast quantities of medical equipment and supplies to North and South Vietnam, the League offered to help both societies with their emergency work. The Republic of Vietnam Red Cross accepted the offer. The nurses, who were recruited by the national societies, gave free medical attention to thousands of people. Small motor boats, painted white with a red cross on the roof, were fitted out as floating dispensaries and transported them along the waterways of the Mekong Delta to visit the people living in isolated areas.

The creation of newly-independent states in Africa provoked many disturbances from 1959 onwards; and in the four years from 1960, six hundred and fifty thousand people were driven from their homes. The High Commissioner for Refugees turned to the League of Red Cross Societies to give emergency assistance to refugees in Togo, those from Angola in the Congo, and other refugees from Rwanda who made their way into Tanzania, Uganda, Burundi and the Kivu Province of the Congo.

The traditional hospitality shown by all African peoples did not fail those refugees; but none of the countries which had so generously and spontaneously harboured them had the resources to support them for any length of time. Often beset with their own problems, the host countries were unable to meet the refugees' needs without help from the United Nations High Commissioner and the Red Cross.

Early in September 1961, two teams of Red Cross delegates with several large crates of baggage left Geneva in specially chartered planes bound for Pokhara. This marked the prelude to an unusual refugee operation undertaken by the International Committee of the Red Cross.

Besides the two doctors who led the expedition, the teams included farmers, an architect, experts in forestry and cultivation, cookery and domestic science, and a secretary. The wide range of goods they took with them might well have puzzled anyone who associated the neutral arm of the Red Cross exclusively with the theatre of war, bandages, medicines and surgical supplies. These, indeed, formed part of the consignment, but it included vaccines for animals and humans, veterinary and dental instruments; blood transfusion outfits; tools for carpenters, joiners, stonemasons, builders and bricklayers; lengths of timber and water-piping; implements for use in a saw-mill and a smithy; cheese-making equipment; land-survey and soil-testing instruments, wireless components, laboratory installations, and cooking and camping materials for the use of the teams.

Swiss firms and businessmen had contributed several of the items for this imaginative project to resettle Tibetan refugees on land made available to them by the Government of Nepal; and as there was no Nepalese Red Cross society at the time, the task was undertaken by the International Committee.

The team's destination was a remote valley in Central Nepal, nine thousand five hundred feet above sea-level, enclosed by mountains rising to fifteen thousand feet and with a river flowing through it. The intense cold and heavy falls of snow which lasted from mid-December till the middle of March made the valley uninhabitable for seven months of the year; during the other five its higher slopes provided summer grazing for herds of sheep, goats, cows, buffaloes and horses, brought there every April by some hundred and fifty Nepalese families, who occupied the wooden huts with their mud floors and shingle roofs weighted down with stones, which could be seen dotted about the mountainside. Here and there on the patches of dry ground fringing the river and in a few forest clearings, the Nepalese had planted potatoes and buckwheat.

To the casual observer the wild uncultivated landscape with its brushwood and fragments of rock presented a scene of desolation. To the refugees from western Tibet, it represented the promised land and they were filled with enthusiasm at the prospect of settling down and remodelling their lives in their new surroundings.

Towards the middle of September, after a nine days' trek from Pokhara, two members of the Red Cross teams arrived in the valley to prepare a landing strip for light aircraft, which was to be in constant use in the coming months. They were followed a fortnight later by the rest of their colleagues and twelve Tibetans, who had been trained as joiners at the handicraft centre established by the International Committee in Khatmandu.

The refugees, divided into three groups, bringing with them their two hundred and twenty-two sheep, four hundred and fifty-eight goats, sixty-four yaks, eighty horses, twelve donkeys, twelve mules and thirty dogs, were expected at the end of September. But the first group, in very poor physical condition, did not arrive until November. The second group, also late, had chosen

Roll-call for Tibetan refugees in Nepal. These were of Dropka stock, originating in Western Tibet, where they lived a nomadic life before their resettlement in the Dhor Patan valley

to come by a circuitous route over mountain passes of twelve thousand feet and had been obliged to leave behind their elderly relatives (later to be rescued by the Red Cross). They were followed, shortly afterwards, by the third group. It was not until 9th, December when all the journeys had been completed, that a roll-call was taken and a hundred and fifty-four Tibetan families were registered.

Although the refugees had not been short of food on their travels, their first medical examination revealed the serious effects of the lack of proteins in their diet. In the months that followed they were given a course of vitamin pills and vaccinated for typhoid, para-typhoid, cholera, smallpox and tuberculosis.

Their livestock and animals were also examined. Yaks and dogs were found to be in excellent condition; but most of the horses, donkeys and mules were in such poor shape that they had to be removed to the lower valleys to survive the winter. Goats and sheep were given antibiotic injections for pneumonia.

The refugees had arrived too late to plough and sow before the cold weather set in, and keeping them supplied with the right kinds of food until the first harvest was ready the following September was a great anxiety. For the time being their staple food was rice, large quantities of which were airlifted from Pokhara in the DC3 aircraft; with salt, onions and other fresh vegetables, tea, butter and oil supplementing the diet.

The huts abandoned by the Nepalese herdsmen at the end of August provided the refugees with temporary homes. Meanwhile the Red Cross architect supervised the building of the first model house, made of stone and clay with a sloping roof, an open fireplace and a vent for the smoke to escape. The head of each Tibetan family was given a plot of land; when he had tilled it and built his house on it he and his dependants qualified for Nepalese citizenship. The plots of land were interspersed among the Nepalese summer dwellings; the black-smith's and carpenters shops, hospital and school occupying central positions in the plan of the settlement, which included a *gömpa*, from which two lamas who had accompanied the refugees could give spiritual guidance to their flock.

The Red Cross teams were later joined by a third doctor, another agriculturalist, a temporary vet, nurses, social workers, young farmers and an administrator whose knowledge of co-operative societies would help the community to become self-supporting.

The land-locked Himalayan kingdom of Nepal is a far cry from the clove-scented island of Zanzibar, where the revolution in January 1961 had created the human problem of another minority. Its solution brought together the efforts of the British Red Cross Society, the International Committee, a sultanate, a sheikdom, several charitable organizations in the United Kingdom and the United Nations High Commissioner for Refugees.

The plight of these refugees was revealed by a British Red Cross nurse, who had been sent to carry out relief for the victims of the disturbance in Zanzibar. She discovered the unseaworthy dhows which were being chartered to take Manga Arabs (Zanzibar-born citizens of Arab origin) to Muscat and Oman, their ancestral homeland in the Arabian Peninsula fifteen hundred miles away. The vessels embarking on these voyages, which took from a fortnight to three weeks, were sailing ships; the travelling conditions similar to those of the slave-trading boats of the past. They had insufficient food and water for the passengers and lacked safety equipment and medicines. What rice was carried on board was found to be old and full of weevils. Furthermore, the masters had been obliged to sign an undertaking that on these journeys they would not enter any port until they reached the Persian Gulf.

Driven by fear of their future, the destitute refugees, many of whom were old men, women and children, had accepted the situation and hundreds of them were crowding on to the dhows which, normally, were authorized to carry not more than fifty passengers.

Despite the Red Cross nurse's protests, the vessels were instructed to sail without further clearance. There was little that she could do, especially as the refugees themselves were anxious to leave as soon as possible. But she was able to put on board each dhow a first aid box and some medicines and instruct one of the refugees in their use. Every bottle-fed baby was provided with a basket, soap, a three weeks' supply of tinned milk and a large plastic sheet for protection against rain, and all the children were given Junior Red Cross disaster relief kits.

The nurse also made out lists with the names of passengers, their relatives and where they lived in the country of asylum. The lists were sent to the authorities to warn them of the arrival of the refugees.

For three months the dhows, dangerously overloaded with their human cargoes, continued to leave at fortnightly intervals, the Red Cross nurse supervising their departure and providing the Red Cross amenities on board. At the end of that time the monsoon broke; the winds changed and no more dhows could sail.

It has never been discovered what sufferings the wretched emigrants endured on these perilous voyages; but by some miracle every dhow reached journey's end.

Meanwhile, the Red Cross nurse's pleas for better travelling conditions for the refugees had not gone unheeded. In co-operation with the United Nations High Commissioner for Refugees, ships were chartered to convey the remaining people, for whom passports and visas were obtained. The countries they wished to settle in were formally approached to accept them, made preparations for their reception and were helped with their resettlement.

These efforts on behalf of the Manga Arabs proved yet again that the troubles of a small group of people are as important to the Red Cross as those of the vast numbers it helps.

12

The National Societies in Peacetime

In the beginning the purpose of the relief societies (later to be known as Red Cross, Red Crescent and Red Lion and Sun societies), formed as a result of the Geneva Meeting in 1863, was to provide trained auxiliaries for the medical services of their armies in time of war. But from the first the societies realized that they could best prepare for their essential wartime duties by practical work in time of peace.

The field of their activities was very soon enlarged and continued to grow. It was not, however, until the Covenant of the League of Nations was drawn up in 1919 that Red Cross work in peacetime was recognized for its own sake and without reference to war.

The First World War of 1914–18 was widely believed to have been 'the war to end all wars'; and to secure the world against future conflict and preserve lasting international peace, the victorious powers who drew up the Peace Treaty created the League of Nations, which was joined by three quarters of the countries of the world.

Since war was now to be outlawed, it might have been supposed that there would be no further use for the Red Cross. But its usefulness in peacetime had already been proved and its future was guaranteed by the signatories to the League of Nations Covenant who, under Article XXV, officially agreed 'To encourage and promote the establishment and co-operation of duly authorized voluntary Red Cross organizations, having as purposes the improvement of health, the prevention of disease and the mitigation of suffering throughout the world'.

Yet in spite of these explicitly recognized purposes and the emphasis placed upon peacetime work, the Red Cross never forgot its historic obligations. When war broke out in 1939, a Convention ensuring the better treatment of prisoners of war had been drawn up by the International Committee of the Red Cross and the national societies were prepared and ready to fulfil the purposes for which they had originally been established.

The League of Red Cross Societies (founded in 1919) gave a welcome impetus to the peacetime work of the Red Cross. Co-operation between the national societies was strengthened, new societies were formed and the movement was placed on an international basis, especially in regard to its disaster relief operations.

Although the activities of the national societies differ from one country to another and have a wider, more varied scope in some countries than in others, they are based on identical principles.

The aim of the Red Cross is always to alleviate suffering and distress. It takes the initiative where it sees a gap unfilled and in finding and doing tasks hitherto ignored; withdrawing from the scene once it has served its usefulness, or when government or other competent authorities are prepared to accept responsibility for the work.

Since its earliest days the Red Cross has been a pioneer, and by now has a record for imaginative enterprises which is unsurpassed.

The Canadian Red Cross Outpost Hospitals and Nursing Services, which are provided for newly-settled communities toiling in the bush and mines of Canada's remote frontier regions, and otherwise without medical facilities, are in the true pioneering tradition.

The Outpost Nurses operating the white cottage nursing stations in places far removed from highways or railways are themselves courageous pioneers; their territory often extends over hundreds of square miles of rough country, through which they travel on foot, horseback or skis, by dog-sleigh, boat, car or plane, in all weathers, to bring medical attention to the sick and injured in the outback areas. 'Nurses of the Showshoes Service', as they are sometimes called, must be prepared for emergencies at any hour of the day or night, accepting entire responsibility for the health and welfare of the small groups of people under their care, from dispensing cough mixture to bringing babies into the world, and acting as friends and advisers in times of family trouble.

The Outpost Hospitals, up-to-date, well-equipped and with from ten to twenty beds, are opened for the larger communities where doctors are more readily available. First established by the Red Cross in 1920, they are to be found today scattered across the length and breadth of Canada. But once a community is sufficiently independent to support its own medical facilities the Outpost is handed over. Each year the Red Cross transfers a certain number of these hospitals to community control and opens others in fresh territory.

The Netherlands Red Cross has a number of pioneer activities to its credit. It is the only society to have set up a service for giving medical advice by radio to ships at sea, and to maintain a mothers' milk bank where the

An Outpost Nurse of the Canadian Red Cross tending an injured lumberman

milk is dehydrated and used for premature and delicate babies.

But the best known feature of its work, apart from the Central Blood Transfusion Laboratory in Amsterdam, is its 'ship of happiness', the *J. Henry Dunant*, which was launched amidst scenes of rejoicing at Rotterdam in 1959, a hundred years after the battle of Solferino. The streets of the city were decked with flowers, and Red Cross flags fluttered over the buildings as the people gathered on the quay to watch the dazzling white boat, with the Red Cross emblem prominently displayed on its funnel, set forth on its maiden trip. Since then throughout the summer months each year the ship has sailed along Holland's waterways, giving a week's holiday, organized by the Netherlands Red Cross, to about two hundred chronically sick, bed-ridden patients and children suffering from respiratory diseases. But the boat is primarily intended for use in emergencies. Built from money subscribed by Dutch industrialists and businessmen, the Netherlands Red Cross and the national disaster fund set up after the North Sea Floods of 1953, the ship is fitted out as a floating hospital for seventy patients, or a temporary refuge for a hundred people (its kitchen can serve up to a thousand meals at a time) and in the event of a natural disaster its purpose will be to sail into the stricken area to rescue the sick and injured.

Most of the national societies have planned special services for times of emergency. The German Red Cross in the Federal Republic of Germany has a disaster train with all the necessary equipment for a rescue operation, ready to travel to any part of Europe.

'I.P.S.A.s', their name formed from the initial letters of their title *Infirmières Pilotes Secouristes de l'Air,* are the members of a dramatic emergency service pioneered by the French Red Cross just before the Second World War. The purpose of these parachutist nurses is to fly anywhere, in peace or war, to help save lives in places inaccessible except from the air. There are about seven hundred of them, all volunteers, who have undergone a strenuous training during which they have had to 'jump' at least eight times, once during a night flight, to qualify for their parachutist diplomas. I.P.S.A.s are afterwards employed as military air escorts, air force nurses, hostesses on French civilian airlines and as aircraft pilots. But flying and parachuting are the spectacular side of their work for they undertake prosaic duties on the ground: caring for the widows and orphans of airmen and arranging holiday camps and Christmas parties for the children.

Other national societies have also developed flying services. In 1963 the Red Cross in the Federal Republic of Germany formed a corps, similar to the I.P.S.A.s, for rescuing victims of accidents and natural disasters. The following year twenty members of a parachutists' club in Finland trained in first aid and transporting injured people and offered themselves as a team to undertake this type of work for the Finnish Red Cross.

Some of the national societies operate air ambulances in their daily work. The South African Red Cross Society's air ambulance carries out 'mercy flights' over a vast area, taking the seriously ill to hospital and doctors to patients. A Red Cross air ambulance began work in Kenya in 1950; fifteen Red Cross ambulance planes have been operating in Finland since 1957.

In Norway the Red Cross has converted motor-boats into ambulances, which are linked up with hospitals and doctors by radio-telephone and give a twenty-four-hour service to the people living in the fiords, whose only connexion with the mainland is by boat. The first of these 'water ambulances' was launched at Kristiansund in 1947; its pilot holds a skipper's licence and both he and his assistant are trained first-aiders. Four years later the society provided the inhabitants of Ålesund with a similar boat, the *Samaritan*, which carries on board surgical instruments, anaesthesia and oxygen outfits and can accommodate four beds or eight sitting patients. The boats take about five hundred sick and injured people to hospital each year. Red Cross members accompany them on every journey, except when a doctor and nurse are travelling with a seriously ill patient.

Special ambulances, on call day and night, are used in the first domiciliary oxygen service, inaugurated in 1962 by the Red Cross in the German Federal Republic, for patients suffering from certain lung or heart diseases. Supplied only on doctors' orders, the apparatus is brought to the patient's home and installed by Red Cross workers, who explain the use of the device which eliminates any danger of receiving too much or too little oxygen.

In Bangkok the Thai Red Cross Society's Saovabha Institute with its snake-farm is a unique undertaking. Venom is milked from the snakes every week to produce the large quantities of serum needed in a country where over a thousand cases of snake-bite occur each year. In 1961 when severe floods inundated Burma, serum from the Institute was supplied to the Burmese Red Cross for hundreds of flood victims who were attacked by waves of cobras, vipers and kraits which had been disturbed by the rising waters.

The Finnish society's plastic surgery unit in Helsinki is the only Red Cross hospital of its kind. Over seven hundred and fifty operations a year are performed at the hospital, which trains specialists in plastic surgery. The majority of the patients are young children requiring operations for hare-lip and cleft-palate; after which they are given speech-threapy at a convalescent home.

The centre for young haemophiliacs at St Aban in Savoie, the first and possibly only centre of its kind in the world, was opened by the French Red Cross in 1964, the same year that the Swiss Red Cross held its first summer camp for children with this affliction.

Holidays, outings and summer-camps for sick, elderly and disabled people of all ages are a rapidly growing service of the national societies, especially their Junior sections, who give pleasure to scores of children with whom they spend holidays each year.

The Austrian Red Cross 'Sun Train' has a similar aim to the Netherlands society's 'Ship of Happiness'. Each year it gives about five hundred invalid and handicapped people the opportunity to enjoy their country's beautiful scenery from the windows of the eleven sleeping-cars they occupy on the journeys arranged for them. Doctors, nurses and Red Cross helpers transfer the patients from their wheelchairs and stretchers to the carriages, and travel with them. Other Red Cross members board the train at various stations to serve hot meals, which include special local dishes to tempt the invalids.

Handicapped children are taught swimming and taken sailing on the Baltic from the Red Cross holiday camp at Haff in the Democratic Republic of Germany. Both German societies were among the earliest of the forty or so national organizations which today teach water-safety and provide life-guards and rescue services at bathing resorts, lakes and other places where drowning accidents may occur.

As long ago as 1910 the American Red Cross initiated a formal programme for teaching swimming, extending it four years later to include life-saving. Under the slogan 'Every American a Swimmer and every Swimmer a Life-saver', thousands of people learnt survival-swimming. The increasing popularity of all forms of water sports in the United States prompted the Society, in 1949, to launch a nation-wide water-safety scheme, with instruction in small-craft handling and safety procedures for powered and un-powered sailing boats. Between the wars the society developed remedial swimming for war-wounded servicemen and crippled children, and later devised special courses for firemen, to reduce the heavy loss of life by drowning while fighting ship and dock fires in their restrictive fire-combat clothing.

Since 1932 water-safety and swimming for crippled children have become prominent activities of the Japanese Red Cross, which started them after a member of the society had returned from the United States where he had studied with the American Red Cross.

The growing enthusiasm for winter sports and mountaineering has brought fresh work to the national societies of several countries outside those traditionally associated with these pastimes. Some societies have long been responsible for training mountain guides and ski instructors in first aid and rescue techniques; others provide these services through their own specially trained teams.

The Red Cross Mountain Patrol in the Democratic Republic of Germany is one of the oldest in Europe and has earned a reputation for carrying out dramatic rescues which extends far beyond its natural frontiers. The Patrol members, in addition to their routine tasks, are called to aid workers injured by avalanches and falling rock on roads, construction sites and in quarries. On one occasion fifteen of them cleared sixty tons of rock from a mountain pass blocked by a landslide.

The Norwegian Red Cross has a long established Mountain Safety service. The members, all of whom are expert skiers and conspicuous from a great distance in the bright red anoraks they wear on duty, are trained in

Mountain rescue in the Democratic Republic of Germany

searching for victims, treating winter injuries, moving casualties over glaciers and avalanches and the uses of rope for rescue work. They are equipped with 'walkie-talkie' sets and transport their casualties by dog-team and snowmobile.

Similar services are provided for sportsmen by the Victoria Red Cross Ski Patrol Corps in Australia, where the ski-centres are in remote, unpopulated areas.

In Ecuador the Red Cross *Nuevos Horizontes* team has set up an extensive patrol and rescue service for climbers injured or stranded on their famous mountain, Chimborazo; the Mexican Red Cross team shares its duties with the country's ambulance corps.

With an increasing number of tourists and climbers visiting Mount Halla, a national beauty spot on Cheju Island in the Republic of Korea, the Red Cross decided to organize a mountain rescue team and first aid services, which by now have been in operation for some years.

First aid is associated with the name of the Red Cross all over the world in industry and on the highways, where it was introduced by the national societies of several countries between the two World Wars.

In the United Kingdom the first aid posts set up by the British Red Cross at intervals along the main roads, especially those leading to the coast, are manned by members during summer week-ends and holiday times; and since 1963 the society has made available to motorists special first aid kits and short courses of instruction aimed at giving them the basic information to save lives in road accidents.

Throughout Spain the Red Cross has organized a network of highway first aid centres, to which motorists needing help are directed and accidents reported by Red Cross motor-cyclists, who patrol the national highways from seven o'clock in the morning until ten at night on Sundays and holidays. The centres are staffed by doctors, medical students and nurses and placed at strategic points along the roads. An ambulance is attached to each centre, which is furnished with ophthalmotonometers for examining a motorist's sight, and facilities for checking headlights, brakes, tyres and mechanical faults in cars.

The Italian Red Cross highway first aid posts have dispensaries attached to them and are equipped to carry out minor surgery, administer oxygen and blood transfusions. The teams working at the posts are composed of doctors and volunteers and linked up by radio-telephone with ambulances.

The Red Cross was the originator of first aid in the mines, and since 1920 the South African Red Cross has supervised the safety of mineworkers and taught first aid to over a million people employed in the country's leading industry. In the large mining areas of the Soviet Union first aid posts are established at pit-heads and down the shafts, first-aiders accompanying the new

A Chinese Red Cross member giving first aid to an injured miner

workers on every shift until they have become familiarized with the safety regulations.

The Romanian, Hungarian and Bulgarian societies organize and man first aid posts for labourers during the annual harvest and threshing seasons; attending to accidents, inspecting the supplies of drinking water, sanitary arrangements and the premises where meals are prepared and served. These societies are also responsible for the first aid posts set up in factories, workshops, mines, schools and villages throughout their countries. The Czechoslovakian Red Cross undertakes first aid and emergency services for the workers in the country's large forestry areas.

Work for the blind is a Red Cross responsibility in many countries. The Italian Red Cross maintains a centre in Milan for the detection and treatment of glaucoma; in the Republic of Korea eye operations, especially those for the removal of cataracts, are carried out free through the Red Cross. Many of the national societies teach, and transcribe books into Braille. In 1949 the Australian Red Cross started its library of 'talking books' on gramophone records for blind people, and the Netherlands Red Cross established the first of its five cornea centres, or 'eye banks', in Holland. In the Finnish archipelago the Red Cross provides an ophthalmic ambulance, with an oculist and optician who attend to the eye disorders of elderly people.

The Red Cross societies of Austria, Luxembourg and the two German Republics train guide dogs for the blind; over a hundred of them are sent to all parts of the world each year.

The national societies take an active interest in the welfare of mothers and children, particularly in Asian countries, where the mortality rate of children up to the age of four is about thirty or forty times higher than in Europe. The establishment of a clinic, at which mothers could receive ante-natal and post-natal treatment, and young children medical care, was the first aim of the Cambodian Red Cross after its foundation. The building, equipped with dental and x-ray units, a pharmacy and store, was completed in 1962; the same year that the Pakistan Red Cross opened several maternity centres and began its scheme for training midwifery students in the rural areas. For some time the Indian Red Cross has maintained a flying squad composed of doctors, nurses and stretcher-bearers who are on maternity duty day and night.

First aid in a harvest field in Hungary

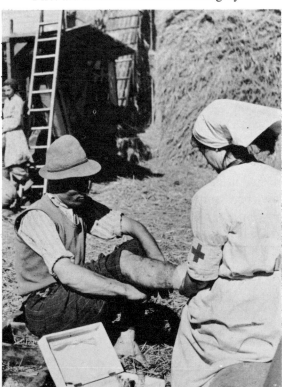

Child welfare is one of the main activities of the Brazilian Red Cross, which administers canteens and has set up a milk-bank for poor children; and of the Colombian Red Cross, which gives pre-natal consultations to mothers and free dental care to the children of the poorer classes. The Danish Red Cross has continued the cot-lending service which it started for needy mothers during the war, and presents a baby's layette to each mother. American Red Cross home-welfare aides work among the Cherokee Indians in North Carolina, the Apache Reservations of Arizona and the Navajo and San Carlos reservations, advising wives and mothers on family budgets, the essentials of a well-balanced diet and care of sick and injured in the home.

Since the Red Cross was born at a time when public conscience had been awakened to general ills, preparing the ground for many advances in social work, it is not surprising that the national societies should have entered the field of social service at the earliest opportunity, organizing and pioneering welfare activities and continuing to meet fresh needs arising out of the changing social conditions.

The large and increasing number of old people has stimulated a wide range of special services undertaken for them by the national societies, which also have established homes, hostels and flatlets for elderly people. By now there are few communities in Britain which do not possess their old people's clubs, a large number of which are run by the Red Cross.

The success of these clubs in overcoming much of the loneliness and isolation of old people, to many of whom they are the only taste of community life they enjoy, led the society to open clubs for the disabled. The modern aim for this section of the community is rehabilitation, with the goal of helping even those who are severely handicapped to lead a life which is as socially and economically independent as possible. The Red Cross clubs for the disabled, to which hospitals and social workers often send discharged patients, have proved equally successful and are almost as numerous as the clubs for old people.

More recently, the national societies have entered the field of mental health; and with the aim of breaking down the apathy and social stigma attaching to this type of illness, visit and organize for the patients many group activities, in hospital and after they are discharged. The British Red Cross plays an active part in an imaginative scheme, started in 1959, for giving beauty treatment to women patients in mental hospitals to encourage them to take a pride in their appearance. Plastic surgery and other long-term patients also benefit from this type of therapy, to which many of the hospitals have given their blessing by opening beauty salons.

The British society's Picture Library scheme, under which reproductions of famous pictures are taken from time to time into the hospital wards where the patients choose which ones they would like hung on the walls, has spread to several countries.

The career of Florence Nightingale, who was already famous by 1863, has been a constant inspiration to the Red Cross movement. Over two hundred and fifty schools of nursing have been established by the national societies which have provided many countries with their first professional nurses. Some of the societies award annual fellowships and scholarships enabling nurses to specialize in their work.

An Indian Red Cross rural nurse on a home visit

What was subsequently to become the first Red Cross school of nursing had a modest beginning at a house in Karlsruhe, where four young women started their training under the patronage of the Grand Duchess Luise of Baden in 1860. Six years later, when war broke out between Austria, Germany and Italy, the pupils and graduate nurses were authorized to wear the white armband with a red cross while caring for the wounded; and all nurses of this school have subsequently worn the Red Cross emblem on their uniforms.

The training in auxiliary nursing given by the national

societies to their volunteers has been of inestimable value to the hospitals, enabling hundreds of nursing members to provide useful help when wards are under-staffed through sickness and epidemics. As well as their hospital duties these members, working under the super-vision of district and rural nurses, care for home-bound sick and infirm people. Each year hundreds of young girls who have joined the Junior sections of their national societies enter the nursing profession.

Mr Oliver's initiative in starting a panel of voluntary blood donors in the British Red Cross society not only influenced medical history but provided a model and inspiration for the creation of similar services throughout the world. The fact that the donors were voluntary and unpaid was in harmony with the tradition of the Red Cross; for though blood is still paid for in some countries, thousands of men and women are daily exemplifying the Red Cross ideal of giving blood 'as the free gift of one man to another in order that his life may be saved'.

Eleven national societies at the time of the centenary of the Red Cross were entirely responsible for the blood transfusion work in their countries; the research laboratories they have established for blood, its products and their uses, are among the leading institutions of their kind in the world. In other countries where a State service operates, the national societies undertake the recruitment of donors and organization of donor-sessions, and help with the collection of blood.

In describing the immense achievements of the Red Cross, the day to day work, whose driving force has always been voluntary effort, is easily overlooked. The men, women and young people in the national societies, carrying out countless humble and unnoticed tasks quietly and unobtrusively, with no thought of recognition or reward, are the successors of the willing helpers at Castiglione. From them Henri Dunant drew his inspiration for the relief societies which today contribute so much to mankind.

13
Disasters and Emergencies

Henri Dunant foresaw numerous opportunities of extending the humanitarian work of the voluntary aid societies once they were established, and as early as 1863, in the third edition of *A Memory of Solferino*, he wrote 'Such societies could even render great service during epidemics, or at times of disaster ... The victims of hunger, fire, and excessive cold, of shipwrecks, and floods, landslides, earthquakes, and railway accidents, cholera, and other epidemics deserve exactly the same attention as the war wounded. These calamities might happen unexpectedly ... Speed is therefore the main concern ...' and he urged that 'groups in constant readiness' should be formed, to give 'the promptest help'.

His words were to show one direction in which the Red Cross was to develop and, in time, become the largest organization of its kind in the world.

At an international Red Cross conference in Berlin in 1869, the societies themselves decided 'To provide assistance and relief in disasters which may afflict peoples during peacetime', subsequently organizing and training their volunteers and setting aside special funds and supplies for these purposes.

Relief to the victims of disasters is a traditional activity of the American Red Cross, which was later appointed by Congress to act as the nation's official relief agency in disasters. The first Red Cross chapter, set up by Clara Barton at Dansville, New York, had been established only a few days when forest fires broke out in Michigan, destroying lives and property, and the new society immediately collected money and clothing for the survivors. Mississippi flood victims were the next to receive help, and in succeeding years floods, tornadoes, a hurricane and a tidal wave made urgent calls upon the Red Cross chapter's services.

The efficiency displayed by the American Red Cross in these undertakings won for it universal esteem. Joel Chandler Harris (the author of *Uncle Remus*) sent by his paper to cover the story of one calamity and expecting to find the Red Cross 'a sort of fussy and contentious affair, running about with a tremendous amount of clatter and flourishing a good deal of red tape', found instead, 'something entirely different from any other relief organization that has come under my observation. Its strongest and most admirable feature is its extreme simplicity ... There is no display ... no needless delay. And yet nothing is done blindly or hastily, or indifferently'.

The American Red Cross maintained its reputation during the ten years from 1950 (reputed to be 'the worst decade of disasters in the nation's recorded history') carrying out over three thousand relief operations and providing food, shelter and long-term assistance to half a million victims in the United States.

The governments of several other countries have made their national Red Cross or Red Crescent societies responsible for the relief measures undertaken in emergencies. At such times the societies may be called upon to provide temporary shelter, clothing and food for the survivors; to distribute relief supplies, trace missing people; receive enquiries from and send information to the victims' relatives; introduce measures to prevent or combat epidemics, recruiting, if need be, the doctors, nurses and other specialists for the task and, since most disasters result in a certain amount of sickness and injury among the people in the affected area, arranging for their medical and nursing care. With their trained members, the national societies are well fitted to give auxiliary help to the professional services.

The first to be called to the scene of a crisis, the Red Cross is often there long after the danger is past; indeed, the vast amount of relief and rehabilitation work it carries out on these occasions is seldom realized by the rest of the world.

It is when disaster strikes on a scale too large for a national society to cope with it single-handed, or when calamities following one upon another, as those caused by the forces of nature have a habit of doing, overwhelm a country and create relief needs which are beyond its resources, that the value of the society's international links is felt.

One of the main purposes in founding the League of Red Cross Societies was to provide a central organization for international Red Cross aid. When a disaster occurs, the society of the stricken country immediately informs the League which, if help is required, launches an international appeal telling the other societies exactly what is needed, thus avoiding delay and duplication. Emergency supplies and equipment can also be rushed to the scene of the disaster from relief warehouses the League maintains in various parts of the world.

The first half of the 1960s found the Red Cross contributing large quantities of relief goods and ministering to the survivors of many calamities. Chile experienced the most destructive disaster when a series of earthquakes towards the end of May 1960, followed within a fortnight by tidal waves, destroyed towns and swept away villages, bringing the number of victims to over eight hundred thousand. Forty-two national societies responded to the League's appeal for antibiotics to stave off the threats of epidemics and money to purchase items such as bedding, cooking utensils and household goods, which were bought in other parts of the country to save time and the cost of transport. Five years later Chile was again devastated by an earthquake; fifty thousand people were made homeless and their immediate needs were quickly met by the Chilean Red Cross, which was authorized to draw supplies from the League's relief warehouse at Santiago. Although the society considered that an international appeal was unnecessary, spontaneous contributions came from several societies, among them the Netherlands Red Cross, whose imaginative gift, Dorro Brando, a dog specially trained in searching for buried victims, was awarded the Canine Defence Medal for finding seven people under a sea of mud in the Chilean mining town of El Cobre.

No natural disasters are more sudden and give their victims less chance to escape than earthquakes. Beside those which shattered vast areas of Chile during these years are others whose names have become household words in the vocabulary of calamities, and recall the relief actions of the national societies.

Red Cross teams were already in Morocco engaged in a relief operation of a highly specialized nature, when the appeal was made by the League of Red Cross Societies on behalf of Agadir. This Moroccan town was destroyed by an earthquake in twelve seconds before midnight on 29th February 1960. The tragedy brought to the scene surgeons, nurses and three hundred and twenty tons of supplies from sixty-one national societies. Red Cross and Red Crescent relief workers set up a tented camp a few miles away from Agadir, and for four months sheltered and cared for ten thousand homeless people. The fine hospital complex of five hundred beds with its laboratory, dispensary and nursing school standing on the outskirts of the once ruined town, was built from the surplus funds after the earthquake and as a monument to the twelve thousand dead and the help given by the Red Cross.

Two years later on the night of 1st September another earthquake, lasting sixty seconds but according to the Seismological Institute at Uppsala a hundred times more violent than that of Agadir, reduced to heaps of rubble seventy-five obscure villages in north-west Persia. Within hours army trucks were driving to the area medical teams and equipment, sent by forty-three national societies. The Red Cross found the most ancient and modern forms of transport expedient to convey the relief materials to the sequestered villages; while planes flew over them dropping urgently needed supplies, scores of donkeys, bought in Teheran, were loaded up with the less essential goods and picked their way over the stony mountain paths to find new owners among the people whose livestock had perished in the earthquake. With winter approaching, the need for homes for the sixty thousand survivors was acute; but many of them were soon helping to construct prefabricated houses from the eight tons of materials and framework flown out from the United Kingdom.

Ten months later Skopje, the third largest city in Yugoslavia, with a population of two hundred thousand, was razed to the ground in fifteen seconds by an earthquake and tremors which continued for several days. The rebuilding of the city was a governmental responsibility. But the Red Cross immediately embarked upon a feeding scheme for six thousand children and nursing mothers, later extending it to include thirty thousand children who for the next nine months were given breakfast, a hot lunch and evening meal each day in tented and prefabricated dining-rooms. Fifty-two national societies contributed towards the project. As the city was without gas, electricity and water supplies the meals were prepared in three mobile kitchens provided by the Red Cross societies of Sweden and the two German Republics.

To describe the many relief operations the Red Cross carried out after natural disasters during these years would be far beyond the scope of this book. Nevertheless, the volcanic eruption which threatened Tristan da Cunha in 1961 stands out for the universal sympathy and concern it aroused for the small, helpless community inhabiting 'the world's loneliest island'.

As soon as it was known that the islanders were to be brought to the United Kingdom, the British Red Cross cabled the South African Red Cross asking it to provide them with any help they might need when they boarded the *ss. Stirling Castle* at Cape Town. The society also arranged that they should be met at Southampton and escorted to Pendell Camp in Redhill, where local Red Cross members awaited them with toys, knitted blankets and other comforts. Other members, in charge of the sick-bays at the camp, were soon busy caring for the new arrivals, most of whom were suffering from colds, bronchitis and the asthma they had inherited from their common ancestor, Corporal Glass.

For the bewildered islanders as they left the warm coaches which had taken them on that cold November afternoon to Pendell, where a bevy of newspaper reporters and cameramen confronted them, the sight of the familiar face of Mrs Vivien Woolley brought tears of joy. They last had seen her seventeen years before, when she left Tristan with her husband at the end of his spell of duty as their doctor. Now a Red Cross officer in Derby, she had travelled south to meet and help them to settle in.

But she was not their only link with the Red Cross; the story of their association is full of charm. About sixteen years separated their arrival in the United Kingdom and the day that a parcel was delivered at British Red Cross headquarters. The parcel contained thirty knitted garments and some tiny sealskin shoes made by the islanders, together with a letter of thanks for the much needed supplies the society had sent them in 1945, at a time when they, perhaps even more than the people of Britain, were feeling the shortages of the post-war years. Until the latter half of the Second World War, when a meteorological station was established on Tristan da Cunha, there was one post a year to and from the island. Thus it was well into 1940 before the islanders heard that war had broken out and the women began knitting for the Red Cross. In course of time their gifts arrived in the United Kingdom and the Red Cross thanked them by the next annual post.

The bonds of friendship were to be strengthened while the exiles were in England. Even though they never overcame their homesickness, declaring stoutly, 'We's going back there as soon as the hould thing has stopped smoking', and two years later when the volcano was pronounced extinct most of them elected to return, the Red Cross officers seeing the islanders off at Southampton said good-bye to fourteen of their children who had been enrolled in the Junior Red Cross.

Grateful as ever three years later, the islanders again sent gifts to the Red Cross. The schoolmaster returning to the United Kingdom on completion of his assignment to Tristan brought with him fifty skeins of white wool, spun and carded by the women after they had sheared the island's five rams. They knew the gift would be welcomed at the Red Cross old people's clubs, where the members knitted the wool into shawls and small blankets for other old people and made infants' garments needed in the Seychelles. The Tristan da Cunha Red Cross juniors sent their own special gift to their former colleagues of the New Forest: a Friendship Album with photographs, drawings and a brief account of their daily life on what must surely be one of the most unexpected places in the world to find the Red Cross emblem.

Natural disasters are not the only occasions on which a national society turns to its fellow societies for aid. Some years ago a mass accident involving the crowd who were watching a torchlight procession to mark the anniversary of Mahomet's death, gave rise to this distress signal to the League of Red Cross Societies:

'GRAVE UNEXPECTED DISASTER BEIRUT—
TWO HUNDRED SERIOUSLY BURNT—
LEBANON REDCROSS ASKS HELP

URGENTLY—HUMAN BLOOD PLASMA—
ANTITETANUS SERUM—BANDAGES—
GAUZE—DEEPLY GRATEFUL'

The flaming torches carried by hundreds of boys and girls partaking in the ceremony had been dipped beforehand in buckets of fuel and all of them had been leaking. One torch, dropped on the petrol-soaked ground, had instantly transformed it into a carpet of fire; scores of young people suffering from burns were rushed into hospital.

The appeal started a rescue operation directed by the League of Red Cross Societies. Within hours blood-plasma and anti-tetanus serum from the Netherlands and Swiss Red Cross societies were despatched by air from Amsterdam and Berne, and nearly a ton of blood-plasma from the Canadian Red Cross arrived at Geneva, where quantities of surgical dressings were picked up and flown to Beirut in United States Air Force planes. Many of the injured required repeated blood transfusions which were made possible through the additional supplies of plasma sent by the Red Cross societies of the German Federal Republic, France, Greece, the Netherlands, Sweden and America; when more anti-tetanus serum was wanted, the Persian Red Lion and Sun society provided it. Within seventy-two hours the needs of all the victims had been met and many lives had been saved.

Sudden calls for help like the one described are frequently received by the national societies which maintain blood transfusion centres and research laboratories in connexion with blood and its derivatives. Sometimes the request is for a rare type of blood.

Some years ago the Canadian Red Cross National

Research Laboratory made medical history by establishing, after long study on an international basis, that twenty-four people in the world had what was probably the rarest of all types of blood, and that twenty-one of them were members of a metis family living in an Iroquois Indian settlement in the backwoods of Alberta. As a result of this discovery and the blood donations of two members of the family, life was later given to a baby whose mother had a rare sub-type of blood, which meant that immediately the baby was born its blood had to be replaced with the same type as that of the metis family. The hospital in California where the baby was expected appealed for help to the American Red Cross, who approached the Canadian Red Cross. A doctor from the Edmonton Red Cross centre set out at once on a thirty-six-mile journey, by station-wagon and hay-wagon and horses over mud-bound roads, to obtain one bottle of the blood; next day travelling thirty miles in another direction to obtain a second bottle. Back at Edmonton he made special preparations to ensure that the blood could be flown at an altitude of thirty-five thousand feet without danger of breaking the bottles. It was then handed to the Canadian Air Force, who flew it by jet plane to Alameda, where it was met by the American Red Cross, inspected by a laboratory technician to confirm that it was still in good condition and, finally, delivered to the hospital by two Red Cross drivers. When the baby girl was born a week later, she was found to be suffering from the dread disease the doctors had anticipated and was given the exchange transfusion which saved her life.

On another occasion a request for blood of a rare type united the efforts of the Australian and Greek Red

Cross societies in obtaining it for a young Greek woman living in Melbourne and expecting her second baby in 1963. Tests before the birth of her first child had identified her with only twenty people in the world whose blood was of the Bombay type (so named because it was there that doctors in 1952 had discovered it) and on that occasion a donor in the United States had provided it. Her family lived in a remote part of southern Greece and samples of their blood, obtained and sent by the Greek Red Cross to the Australian Red Cross, revealed that only her sister had this unusual type. Neither of the two babies did in fact inherit it from their mother, but after her second confinement she gave some of her blood to be stored for use should she need it in the future.

Blood fractionation (that is, the separation of human blood plasma into its chemical components or fractions) undertaken by some national societies, has yielded various substances which have made a spectacular contribution towards saving life. One of these fractions, the immune (*gamma*) *globulin*, which prevents or diminishes the effects of certain virus diseases, was urgently needed in the spring of 1965 when a virulent form of measles swept through the eastern province of Turkey, claiming the lives of over four hundred children. Nine national societies in Europe and North America answered the Turkish Red Crescent's appeal. In addition they sent gifts of food and clothing to be distributed to the inhabitants of the isolated mountain villages, where conditions were made worse by a temperature of minus 30 degrees Centigrade and heavy falls of snow. Within weeks Red Crescent doctors had given the injections to all children between the ages of six months and three years, and the epidemic was halted.

The outbreak of an epidemic often gives rise to a call for Red Cross aid. In 1961 when Ethiopia was suddenly faced with its first yellow-fever epidemic without the necessary vaccine to combat it, the League of Red Cross Societies arranged for twenty thousand doses to be flown from Dakar to Addis Ababa. Two years later the Japanese and Philippines societies came to the rescue of the Republic of Korea with large quantities of vaccine to stem a cholera epidemic which had broken out in six provinces.

The Moroccan disaster, which occured a few months before the Agadir earthquake referred to earlier, was unexpected as it was horrifying, and engaged the Red Cross in a relief operation without parallel in medical history. Nearly ten thousand people (half of them children) living in the Meknes region were stricken with paralysis after cooking their food in vegetable oil adulterated with *tri-ortho-crecyl-phosphate*, a chemical used in manufacturing plastics and present in the synthetic lubricant for turbo-jet engines. Closer investigations disclosed that surplus stocks of the lubricant, no longer required by an air base closing in the area, had fallen into the hands of a gang of racketeers who made a profitable business by mixing it with vegetable oil and selling it in goatskins, whence it made its way into the small dark kitchens of the stricken population and its cloudy appearance remained undetected.

Most of the victims lost the use of their hands or legs, or both; in the severer cases the spinal cord was affected. Physiotherapy at an early stage was a vital factor in their recovery and in limiting the extent of the paralysis.

The specialist care and treatment of so large a section of the population placed a heavy burden on this small country, which was already giving asylum to nearly a hundred and twenty thousand Algerian refugees; they had only seventeen thousand hospital beds (soon to be further reduced by the Agadir earthquake) and their Red Crescent society had been established less than two years.

National societies immediately recruited doctors, nurses and physiotherapists and flew them to Casablanca. Over a thousand beds, linen, blankets, food and clothing and two field hospitals, each equipped with four hundred beds for use in the rural areas, were carried in aircraft provided by several governments at the request of their national societies.

Factories, garages and casernes in Morocco were hastily turned into treatment centres and, for the paralysed children, a former barracks was converted into a hospital, with facilities for them to receive some schooling as they recovered. A fleet of vehicles was organized to bring their parents to visit them, and for the use of the many patients whose only means of getting to the five treatment centres from the outlying districts was in carts, on donkeys, or on bicycles pushed by members of their families. As most of the patients were illiterate, they were issued with red or green cards to match the colours of the trucks which were to take them to the centres in the mornings or afternoons.

Their reluctance to undergo treatment, especially when it meant separation from their families, was gradually overcome. As once useless limbs returned to normal, indifference changed to enthusiasm, often bringing patients to the centres on days when they were not expected and long after they had been discharged.

In spite of the innumerable difficulties of language,

climate, working with unfamiliar equipment or improvising it when there was none, the Red Cross teams, in addition to treating the paralysis victims, trained Moroccan medical students, nurses and social workers in physiotherapy, so that they would eventually be able to hand over to them. Brace shops were also set up where skilled artisans were taught to make orthopaedic appliances, crutches and walking-sticks.

It soon became evident that the relief undertaking would have to be prolonged. Patients who had been pronounced cured required testing and re-examining at regular intervals to make sure that their recovery was

A Red Cross physiotherapist helping a paralysed Moroccan woman to learn to walk again

complete. For those who had lost their former employment through their disability, or who would never recover, some form of rehabilitation would have to be devised. In the months that followed occupational therapy centres were opened, where these people were taught their traditional village crafts of embroidery, blanket and carpet weaving, copper and leatherwork and employed in making winter clothing for the Algerian refugees. With the work done at these centres a new attitude of mind was created towards the disabled person, recognizing his right to earn a living and support his family and the duty of the community to help him to attain this goal.

When the Red Cross teams finally withdrew in the summer of 1961, over nine thousand formerly paralysed people had been cured, with about seven hundred still requiring treatment regularly or periodically.

Not for the first time had the Red Cross gone to the aid of a country in distress leaving it better equipped to alleviate suffering in the future: the foundation of the first training school for physiotherapists in North Africa was the lasting memorial to the twenty months the teams had spent in Morocco.

For the paralysis victims the help of experts and professionals was required and these were recruited for the task by the Red Cross: what the survivors in the small Welsh mining village of Aberfan chiefly needed, when tragedy entered their lives on Friday 21st October 1966, was the practical sympathy of Red Cross members; ordinary men and women, many of whom, like themselves, were parents and housewives in everyday life, and whose Red Cross training had taught them how to act in an emergency.

The appalling death-roll of a hundred and forty-four

shocked the entire world, especially as a hundred and sixteen were young children attending the infant and junior school, which was to have closed for the half-term holiday three hours after the building was engulfed by the avalanche of black slurry, sweeping down the mountainside from the eight-hundred-foot high, water-logged coal tip overlooking the village. Faced with the horrifying spectacle of this disaster it would have been easy to panic; but the Red Cross helpers knew what to do and quickly and efficiently began their work.

They set up a first aid post for the rescue-workers, to whom they also gave out hot drinks and snacks from a van drawn up on the site of the avalanche; they opened and manned first aid and information posts elsewhere in the village; they distributed relief supplies, food and replacements of household goods to those whose homes had been destroyed; they cared for the grief-stricken parents throughout the long hours of watching and waiting in the blinding sleet and rain. As the bodies of the victims were recovered, they helped the stretcher-bearers to take them to the temporary mortuary, where their most exacting task—entrusted solely to the Red Cross—continued night and day until its completion. Some helped to dig graves and engrave coffin-plates, others sorted and labelled the hundreds of wreaths and flowers which began to arrive for the mass funeral towards the end of the week.

Before long the Red Cross members were joined by others from the Midlands and West of England; altogether nearly eight hundred of them gave their services, working in eight-hour shifts of thirty at a time.

The Red Cross continued its compassionate work for several months afterwards. Quietly and unobtrusively each week-end, bereaved families from the stricken village were flown to Guernsey for short holidays—the airline and hotel-keepers giving them free air passages and accommodation—during which the island's Red Cross was able to look after them.

The offers of help received from the other national societies after this disaster showed yet again the good-will that exists between them, and their recognition of the fact that it is their duty to help one another. There has, indeed, not been an occasion when the League of Red Cross Societies has appealed for assistance when national societies have not come to the aid of a fellow society. Sometimes strong differences of political opinion have existed between the countries helping and being helped; but undeterred by them all national societies have considered the victims overcome by misfortune, irre-spective of their race, or creed, or political views.

14

The Junior Sections

The Spanish children who begged to be allowed to join the Red Cross in 1867 and, indeed, Mrs Mackinnon of Australia who formed the first junior sections about fifty years later, would have been amazed to learn that by 1963 when the Red Cross celebrated its centenary, over seventy million young people were enrolled in the movement.

Since 1920 when the General Council of the League of Red Cross Societies resolved at its first meeting 'that a National Red Cross Society should organize the youth of its country for Red Cross service', the Junior Red Cross has gone from strength to strength, increasing not only in numbers but the variety and scope of its work.

Its objects, 'to inspire young people with the spirit of the Red Cross and to provide them with the opportunities of Red Cross service', proved their effectiveness in the Congo in 1960. The national society had not then been established; but as the chaos in the country mounted, the Congolese juniors, who had been trained by the Belgian Red Cross, rose to meet the crisis, assuming responsibility for and carrying out reliably and impartially tasks usually undertaken by adults. In Kasai Province juniors from the Baluba and Lulua, tribes that were hostile to each other, worked side by side doing relief work; the juniors of the one tribe sometimes intervening between their own tribal members on behalf of

Milk for Congolese children

the juniors of the other. The delegate of the International Committee of the Red Cross, who stepped out of the plane at Leopoldville airport into a confused mass of harassed officials and frightened refugees huddled together waiting to leave the country, was heartened to see the band of smiling boys and girls who immediately recognized and greeted him. Many of them were trained first-aiders and had come forward to offer their help long before the appeal for it was made. When violence broke out these young people, some of whom were no older than fifteen, realized, as Henri Dunant had at Solferino, that medical aid for the wounded must somehow be organized and emergency care be given to the civilian victims of the fighting. They braved the firing lines to rescue the injured (three juniors lost their lives in their attempts) and collected and buried the dead. They re-opened abandoned dispensaries, arranged transport for expectant mothers, took food and water to prisoners who had been without either for several days and success-fully appealed to the authorities to allow detainees who were seriously ill to be admitted to hospital. As sick and injured hostages who had been rescued from Stanley-ville arrived at Leopoldville airport, teams of juniors transferred them from the planes; and from the special centres which had been established in the capital and other cities they distributed milk, sugar and vitamin tablets to eighty thousand children a day. Later when an outbreak of smallpox threatened the Bas Congo (where many Angolan refugees had settled) they worked with the health authorities in a mass vaccination campaign.

The three aims of the Junior Red Cross, 'the protection of life and health, service to the sick and suffering and international friendship and understanding', are the framework of all its activities around the world.

Combining the first and second of these aims, Lebanese juniors carried out an ambitious health project, which transformed the primitive village of Saaydeh into a model for the other villages buried in the same backward region of the country. With the support of the authorities who selected Saaydeh for this pilot scheme, the American

University in Beirut, engineers, builders and merchants who volunteered their help and gave the materials, forty juniors, joined each day by a busload of their companions, moved into the village. During the next ten days they levelled the ground, mixed concrete, built walls, erected fences and cleared a space to lay out a small public garden. The installation of washrooms and kitchens in the houses gave the seventy families their first real chance to overcome the dirt and disease they had hitherto known. Having completed the reconstruction of the village, the juniors went on to teach the children basic hygiene and held courses in health and simple home-nursing for the women, after which Junior Red Cross leaders, first-aiders and nurses visited Saaydeh for several weeks to continue the instruction.

Juniors of the Soviet Union played a prominent part in a nation-wide anti-poliomyelitis campaign which was so successful that the disease has been eradicated in Esthonia and other territories.

In isolated and developing countries where the shortage of medical and social services is acute, junior sections are undertaking health education, tackling the problems of disease and ignorance which are prevalent among the population. Malaria, which is still the major health hazard of many tropical and sub-tropical countries, was stamped out in a mountain village in Guatemala, where it was claiming more victims every day until the young members reported it to the authorities, who taught them how to use the special equipment to spray all standing water in and near the village. In the Republic of Korea, juniors have campaigned against the age-old fear of leprosy and regularly visit leper colonies; in New Guinea, by persuading the tribe in one village to break with the ruthless tradition of casting out old people to fend for themselves once they have become too old to work, the juniors have dissuaded the tribes in other villages from disposing of their old people in this way. At first the elderly outcasts were reluctant, but eventually agreed to accept the fruit and vegetables the juniors had grown for them in their school gardens. When their Australian colleagues heard of the enterprise, they rather pertinently asked how the old people would fare before the produce was ripe and promptly 'adopted' the New Guinea group, supplying them with all that they needed.

Canadian juniors decided upon dental care as one of their health projects and, well known in Red Cross circles for their ingenious forms of help and the distance it travels, raised the money to provide Newfoundland with a 'floating dental clinic'. All through the summer months the dentist in charge and his wife, who is a trained nurse and acts as his assistant, call at the ports along the one-hundred-and-ninety-mile stretch of coastline to give the people free treatment, which they continue to receive during the winter when he travels by snowmobile provided also by the juniors. In Ontario, for the hundreds of scattered communities which are too small to support resident dentists, they purchased the first 'Dentist on Wheels' (a mobile unit combining a clinic and accommodation for the dentist and his family) which went into action in 1948, and later paid for two additional units to serve this province of over four hundred square miles. These travelling dentists make their way to the schools where they may remain for weeks, or months, depending on the size of the district, and are very popular with the five thousand children whose teeth they inspect each year.

More recently the Canadian groups supplied Eskimos with emergency medical packs to use on their hunting and fishing trips in areas remote from medical facilities.

Czechoslovakian groups have launched a drive to improve the health of gipsy children; New Zealand groups sponsor children sent to convalesce in Swiss sanatoria.

A nation, it has been said, often shows its true greatness by its regard for its weaker members; and the second of the Junior Red Cross aims, 'service to the sick and suffering', gives young people almost unlimited opportunities to help their own immediate countrymen and develop a sense of responsibility towards those less fortunate than themselves. Even in countries where the social services are highly developed there are countless ways in which the lives of the elderly and handicapped can be eased and made a little brighter. In Britain during the severe winter of 1963, juniors were to be found bringing in the coals (often supplied by the State service) for old people and sweeping the snow from the paths leading up to their doors. At other times, they push them in their wheelchairs to church, or out shopping; run errands for them, collect their prescriptions from the chemists, their books from the libraries and carry out a host of other kind deeds for them. The aim of service was charmingly interpreted by two very young members who, on their way to and from school each day, called at the house of an old couple to change their shoes and slippers. In Stuttgart fifty per cent of the fatal street accidents befell old people until the local Red Cross juniors of this German Republic gave them traffic drill.

Services to the blind occupy a place in the programmes of most sections. Italian juniors translate books and

A Junior Red Cross member talking to a deaf-blind woman,
using the manual language—and many a joke is shared

magazines into Braille and record 'speaking' text-books
for blind students; British juniors learn the manual
language which makes them conversable visitors at the
homes of deaf–blind people and agreeable companions
on the outings arranged for them. Many blind children

in Austria are encouraged to take a more active part in social life and increase their independence and self-reliance by learning a sport at which they can become equally adept with their sighted instructors of the Austrian Junior Red Cross. Thus the admiring crowd, who watched the two children figure-skating on an ice-rink in Vienna, would not have known that one of them was blind, the other the junior who had taught her. Special draught-boards, with the squares in relief and differently shaped to enable the blind player to distinguish between the black and the white, are made by the juniors, and maps, using papers of different textures to indicate the various colours, are prepared for blind children. In summertime there are excursions for them to the Vienna woods, and nature-rambles on which they feel and learn the names of the flowers, leaves and other specimens the juniors collect for them.

Summer heralds the annual holidays for handicapped children, a particularly happy junior activity in several parts of the world. A young member is detailed to be a playmate and helper to each child and everyone shares in the chores and fun. The holidays have a three-fold purpose: they give the young helpers an opportunity to put their training into practice, the parents of the handicapped child a well-earned rest, and the child himself companionship of his own age and the chance to develop his personality and extend the range of his activities. It is often on one of these holidays that a disabled child, away from the over-protection and parental anxiety normally surrounding him, discovers he can do something new which formerly he had thought was beyond him, and perhaps for the first time something he can do for some one else. When two severely handi-

A blind child with a Red Cross junior, at a summer holiday
camp

capped boys, who had spent holidays with the British
Red Cross on former occasions, undertook the care of
an eighteen-year-old deaf and dumb spastic boy, sharing
his tent and helping him throughout the ten days of his
holiday, it was an achievement not only for them but
for the British Red Cross who had set them the example
of helping others.

From these holidays developed another activity of
British juniors, who felt it was a pity that the friendships

formed between them and their guests should be dropped when a holiday was over. The clubs, at which disabled young people regularly meet on equal terms with able-bodied juniors and the younger members of senior detachments, provided the answer.

Holidays for invalid and delicate children are a feature, too, of the Austrian juniors' summer programme, and every year since 1956 they have organized for young diabetics a month's stay at their Red Cross home in Mariazell. While there, the children undergo one of the two medical checks they require each year. What has now become an annual event for Swiss invalid children began in June 1965, when twenty small patients from the orthopaedic hospital in Lausanne were helped on to the new 'Friendship Bus' bought by Swiss juniors, who waited with gifts and refreshments for their guests, at all the stopping places along the route taken by the bus past lakes and mountain villages. Several of the children were leaving the hospital for the first time since their admission, and it was scarcely surprising that one of them burst into tears when the outing was over.

Netherlands juniors help to look after the sick, disabled and elderly people on board the society's famous holiday boat, the *J. Henry Dunant*, or staying at the house named after him at Zeist, which they and the young members from the national societies of several European countries built as a token of gratitude for the help received at the time of the North Sea floods.

When this grim tragedy overtook the country, the juniors workèd side by side with their adult colleagues in the rescue and relief operations. Elsewhere they share with the senior members of their societies other exacting tasks which demand speed and clear thinking. In the

Federal Republic of Germany where the Red Cross uses telecommunications in disasters and emergencies, juniors act as radio-telephone operators transmitting the messages; in Italy they drive the flying squad ambulances for the society's emergency home service.

Disasters and their aftermath most often give junior sections the opportunities to express their sympathy and understanding for those who have suffered, the League of Red Cross Societies informing them of the specific needs of the young people. But whether the request is for milk for Algerian refugee children (junior sections in various parts of the world supplied this for three consecutive years) or clothing outfits, recreational and educational materials for Hungarian children in the refugee camps in Austria (two appeals, each for entirely different items, were made to the sections within the short space of three months), the response is always prompt and generous.

At one time among the relief supplies shipped to a country after a disaster there were usually to be found toys, books and games, sent by junior sections to replace those that the young owners had lost. But in 1959 a standardized disaster relief kit was devised for them to prepare and have ready to send to the children who had lost their possessions. Each kit contains sixteen carefully thought out items to provide a child with the basic necessities for eating, washing and playing, and is made of materials which will not break in transit or perish if kept in store: the mug, for example, is of flexible plastic

British Red Cross junior. This child, a victim of poliom-itis since the age of three, was able with her courage to lp other handicapped children at the Red Cross Club and the notebook has no metal spiral binding to rust. The washing things are separately enclosed in a plastic bag to prevent them, once they are in use, from making the rest of the contents of the kit damp; the ball and small toy help the child to while away the long hours spent in a camp or temporary shelter. Any kits that have not been used within a year are offered to the national societies who have not the resources for making them, or need them for their normal welfare and relief work.

Two years later, an appeal to British juniors to 'Drop everything and knit quickly!' had lasting results. Their *Freezing Cold* scheme was launched to provide blankets made of knitted squares for the ninety thousand Algerian refugee children in Morocco and Tunisia, many of whom were spending their fifth year in tents, caves and make-shift huts, during what proved to be an exceptionally hard winter. Knitting fever spread rapidly, and once caught proved to be incurable. The making of blankets has far outlived its original purpose and become a perm-anent activity, and quantities of them are sent each year from Britain to selected countries overseas.

'International friendship and understanding', embody-ing the third of the juniors' aims, is not limited to times of crisis. Another scheme launched by the League of Red Cross Societies has spread a vast network of help from the sections of the older-established societies to their colleagues in several parts of the world, providing them with the materials they require to extend and develop their work. Health kits went from the Netherlands groups to Peru, Togo and Tunisia; school-chests from the German Federal Republic to the Republic of Korea, the Philippines and northern Greece, and from the Canadian to the Turkish groups affected by the earthquake in 1964.

From Luxembourg, equipment was sent to juniors in Morocco, Cameroon and Upper Volta, to whom also cases of gifts have been sent by Japanese groups. The list is inexhaustible and grows longer with the passage of time.

As a school teacher once remarked, 'Geography takes on an added meaning for young people in the Red Cross,' and often a foreign town is not merely a place on a map, but the destination of a Friendship Album which one group is preparing to exchange with another from the group there. The albums passing between the paired groups contain pictures, photographs, pressed flowers, descriptions of their daily lives at home and school, national customs and traditions, special events and something about their Red Cross work. They are the links in the chain of international friendship which is encouraged between all junior sections. The international study centres held in different countries during the summer holidays likewise cement the friendship, bringing together young members of some twenty national societies to discuss their work and exchange ideas, as well as enjoy the entertainments and visits to places of interest in the neighbourhood.

A service project originated by the British Red Cross Society in 1962 takes this a stage further, enabling young people to spend the time between leaving school and going up to a university or taking up a career in doing voluntary work with a national society overseas. Many of these volunteers have helped with distributions of relief supplies and emergency feeding schemes in countries where famine or food shortages exist, taught first aid and hygiene and worked in centres for invalid children. While the scheme was still in its infancy British and Swedish juniors spent several months in the Bahamas, Honduras, Kenya, Singapore, the Solomon Islands, Malawi and Nigeria.

Although the junior organization has its own aims and objects, the training the young members receive and the activities they carry out are designed to fit them for adult membership of their national societies.

This brief account of the practical and useful activities of the national junior sections would be less than complete without some examples of the acts of heroism which have placed the individual members who performed them among the finest exponents of 'the spirit of the Red Cross'. Many juniors have been decorated for bravery; some, like the young Congolese already mentioned, have lost their lives in attempting to save the lives of other people.

One of these was Jeanne Rombaut of Liège, a thirteen-year-old Belgian junior, who was known and loved by all the children in her neighbourhood. One Sunday afternoon, she had taken five of them for a treat to the cinema; the building caught fire and thirty-nine people were burnt to death. In the panic and confusion Jeanne managed to grab four of the children, pushing them towards the doors and outside to safety. But as they neared the exit, she realized that one of them was missing and immediately re-entered the blazing auditorium to look for her. Jeanne's body was later found with a hand extended towards the child she had gone back to save. Jeanne was posthumously awarded the Carnegie Hero Fund's Gold Medal; the Belgian Minister of Education paid homage to her in a message which was read in schools throughout the country; her own, at which she had been an outstanding pupil, was renamed after her and she was formally honoured by the City Council of Liège.

Another junior, Manuelita de la Cruz Donado, in memory of whom a life-saving post bearing her name stands in Puerto Colombia, was eighteen in November 1955 when she volunteered with a group of other Red Cross workers to take food, clothing and medical aid to a small community stranded after the Magdalena river overflowed bringing Colombia its worst floods for many years. For three weeks Manuelita carried out her task with tireless devotion. Then one night the boat in which she was travelling capsized and she was never seen again.

A flooded river also features in the story of Fa'afaga, aged twelve, a West Samoan junior whose courage was twice tested in the fast flowing waters of the Vaisigano, on two consecutive days. A group of terrified children watched her dive into the river and strike out towards a three-year-old boy who was rapidly being carried downstream towards a waterfall and certain death. Fa'afaga was almost exhausted when she caught up with him and, clutching at an overhanging vine, hauled him to safety on the bank. Next day she repeated her act of heroism, rescuing another child from drowning in the same part of the river and for her bravery received the Bronze Medal of the Royal Humane Society of New Zealand.

15
Towards the Unity of Nations

The Red Cross has come a long way since Solferino; yet it cannot even now be said to have reached its final stage. As its history so far has shown, it is no static organization but a movement; forward-looking, adapting itself to modern times and, as a pioneer, often in advance of them.

The inspiration of Henri Dunant is to be found behind every new development of the Red Cross, which has increased its prestige and guaranteed its future, and is a tribute to his genius.

The national societies are the answer to the question he posed in *A Memory of Solferino*; but from the first he envisaged for them tasks lying outside the work assigned to them in war, ensuring their usefulness at all times.

He was looking beyond the care of the wounded of the battlefield to the relief of the victims of natural and other disasters when he wrote, 'To encourage the idea of solidarity between nations in doing good is to oppose war'. He saw clearly that bringing them together to help one another was the most practical means of promoting international friendship and generating the spirit of peace among them.

By the time the reader scans these pages disaster will again have struck in several parts of the world. Aircraft and ships will have carried supplies, and perhaps teams of helpers from the national societies to aid the victims; and the neutrality of the Red Cross, which on the one hand prevents it from taking part in political matters and therefore from taking part in direct action to stop wars, will on the other hand have enabled the national societies to give help outside their own countries. It is, in fact, the societies' complete freedom from racial, political or religious bias which particularly fits them to carry out their work of international relief.

This, and the Junior Red Cross which unites young people throughout the world in their common aim to foster 'international friendship and understanding', are the movement's missions for peace; and no less great for being indirect.

But first and last the Red Cross rests upon the ideal which Henri Dunant set before the world at Castiglione: that a suffering human-being shall be helped for his own sake, without regard for his race, or creed, or political beliefs; above all, whether he is a friend or an enemy. This is a precept which is acceptable to all nations and has withstood the test of time.

The principle of the Red Cross created a spirit of peace in the midst of hatred and dissension at the height of a conflict, over a hundred years after the battle of Solferino, when an Australian Red Cross doctor and his assistant found themselves defenceless and cut off from all communication with the rest of the world. The people around them were hostile and suspicious; the idea of service without reward was new to them and they could not understand why strangers from other countries should want to help them.

Calling together the army leaders, the doctor stipulated that medical care must be given to the wounded of both sides. 'With no means of enforcing our terms, we hardly expected them to be observed,' he later reported, 'but we had absolutely no trouble.' It was his greatest achievement; the belligerents had accepted the principle of the Geneva Convention.

Working in conditions not dissimilar to those after Solferino, the doctor and his assistant treated soldiers of the national army, enemy tribesmen and Tunisian troops of the United Nations forces 'all side by side'; performing operations often without electric light and the usual means of sterilization.

Above the building fluttered an improvised flag made from torn up red curtains and a white sheet; visible to all, respected by all—the emblem of that ideal which has brought the Red Cross to its strength and greatness.

The photographs in this book appear by courtesy of the British Red Cross Society, the International Committee of the Red Cross and the League of Red Cross Societies, except those on pages 10 (Boissonas, Geneva), 30 and 32 (Radio Times Hulton Picture Library), 66 (Keystone Press Agency Ltd.), 166 (Associated Newspapers Ltd.), 171 (Graham Studios), 176 and 178 (Daily Mirror).

Bibliography

J. Henry Dunant   A MEMORY OF SOLFERINO
Cassell & Co (1947). *Translation from the French of the first edition published 1862. Copyright American National Red Cross*

Ellen Hart   MAN BORN TO LIVE
Gollancz (1953)

Fernand Gigon   THE EPIC OF THE RED CROSS OR THE KNIGHT ERRANT OF CHARITY
Jarrolds (1946)

Gustave Moynier   THE RED CROSS: ITS PAST AND ITS FUTURE
Cassell, Petter, Galpin & Co (1883)

Marcel Junod   WARRIOR WITHOUT WEAPONS
Cape (1951)

P. G. Cambrey &   RED CROSS & ST JOHN WAR HISTORY
1939–1947
G. G. Briggs   (1949)

Max Huber   THE RED CROSS
A. Kundig Press: Geneva

Henri Coursier   THE INTERNATIONAL RED CROSS
International Committee of the Red Cross, Geneva (1961)

THE RED CROSS AND THE REFUGEES
Published by the United Nations High Commissioner for Refugees on the occasion of the centenary of the Red Cross
NEWS REVIEW OF THE BRITISH RED CROSS SOCIETY *The monthly magazine of the British Red Cross Society* (*London*)
PANORAMA *The monthly publication of the League of Red Cross Societies* (*Geneva*)
HANDBOOK OF THE INTERNATIONAL RED CROSS
Geneva

Index

Aberfan, 167–9
Abyssinian Red Cross, 62, 63, 64
Agadir, 157
Algerian Refugees in Morocco and Tunisia, 23, 121–4, 126, 165, 167, 181, 182
Alliance of Red Cross & Red Crescent Societies of the USSR, 23–4, 109, 145–6; Juniors, 173
American Red Cross, 34, 50, 56, 57, 58, 87, 108, 141, 148, 153–4, 161, 162; Juniors, 57, 58, 104
Anglo-American Ambulance, 31
Australian Red Cross, 143, 146, 162–3, 187–8; Juniors, 56, 57, 173–4
Austrian Red Cross, 48, 141, 146; Juniors, 104, 177, 179

Bad Pyrmont, 102–3
Barton, Clara, 33–4, 50, 56, 154
Belgian Red Cross, 21, 97, 170
Blood, Appeals for, 59, 160–1, 161–2, 162–3
Brazilian Red Cross, 148
British Red Cross, 29–30, 31–3, 35, 38, 45–7, 50–5, 58, 59–60, 64, 75, 78, 85–7, 89–91, 91–4, 96, 97–8, 99–100, 101, 102–3, 104–5, 109, 111, 112, 113, 131 133, 144, 148–9, 149, 158–60, 167–9; Juniors, 104, 160, 175 176, 178, 178–9, 180, 181–2, 183–4

Bulgarian Red Cross, 109, 114, 146
Burmese Red Cross, 140

Cambodian Red Cross, 147
Canadian Red Cross, 109, 136, 137, 161–2; Juniors, 57, 104 174, 175, 182
Chilean Red Cross, 156
Chinese Red Cross, 109, 110, 145
C-International Ships, 77–8
Civilians in War, Services to, 34, 66, 67, 68–9, 70, 71, 73, 77, 81, 82–3, 85, 88, 89, 90, 90–1, 91–2, 92, 92–4, 105–6, 125, 126
Colombian Red Cross, 148
Committee of Five, 18–19, 20, 26, 28, see International Committee of the Red Cross
Commune of Paris, The, 38–41
Concentration Camps, 71, 83, 95 97
Congolese Juniors, 170–2
Czechoslovakian Red Cross, 104, 146; Juniors, 175

Danish Red Cross, 48, 109, 110, 148
Davison, Henry P., 58
Disaster Relief Kits, 132, 181–2
Displaced Persons, 97, 97–9, 104, 112, 126
Donado, Manuelita de la Cruz, 185

Dunant, Jean Henri, 7–16, 17–22
26, 28, 29, 36, 37–45, 46, 47
48, 95, 103, 107, 137, 152, 153,
179, 186, 187
Dutch Red Cross, 22, 48; *see* Netherlands Red Cross

Ecuador Red Cross, 143
Egyptian Red Crescent, 60
Epidemics, 49, 50, 56, 153, 163,
164

Fa'afaga, 185
Finnish Red Cross, 60, 87, 139,
140, 146
French Red Cross, 22, 28, 31, 32
33, 37, 38, 39, 40, 49, 50, 58,
124, 138–9, 140, 161
Friendship Albums, 160, 183

Geneva Conventions, 7, 8, 26–8
29, 33, 38, 62, 64, 65, 71, 72,
73, 75, 79, 81, 87, 88, 94, 105
–6, 135, 188
Geneva Meeting, 19, 20, 21,
German Red Cross, 30, 31, 32–3,
34, 48, 49, 50, 87, 99, 102, 150;
German Democratic Republic,
141, 142, 143, 146, 158.
Federal Republic, 138, 139,
140, 141, 146, 158, 161;
Juniors, 175, 181, 182
Guatemala Juniors, 173

Hague Conventions, 45, 47, 55,
72
High Commissioner for Refugees, 114, 115, 119, 120, 121–2,
127, 131, 133
Hungarian Red Cross, 109, 113,
117, 146, 147
Hungarian Uprising, 116–121,
181

Indian Red Cross, 110, 147, 150
Inter Arma Caritas, 88
International Committee of the

Red Cross, 18–19, 19–20, 28,
34, 36, 55, 60, 61, 62, 65, 66,
69–70, 72, 74, 75, 76, 77, 78,
79, 80, 81, 82, 83, 88, 89, 94–
5, 97, 104–5, 105–6, 109, 113,
115, 116, 117, 118, 126, 127–
8, 129, 130, 131, 135
Irish Red Cross, 100; Juniors,
104
Italian Red Cross, 48, 49, 50,
58, 60, 110, 145, 146; Juniors,
104, 175–6

Japanese Red Cross, 49, 58, 142
164
Jordan Red Crescent, 105
Jorden, Ella, 111–3
Junior Sections, 56, 103, 120,
123, 151, 170, 172, 173, 175,
176, 177, 178, 179, 181, 182,
183, 184, 187
Junod, Marcel, 60, 61–9, 76, 77,
79–80, 84, 97

Kenya Red Cross, 139
Korean Red Cross, 107; Democratic People's Republic, 108,
110; Republic of Korea, 108,
110, 111, 144, 146; Juniors,
173, 182

League of Nations, 63, 64, 115,
134–5
League of Red Cross Societies
58, 105, 109, 115, 116–7, 119,
120, 121, 126, 135, 155, 156,
157, 160–1, 164, 170, 181, 182
Lebanese Red Cross, 160–1;
Juniors, 172–3
Loyd Lindsay, V.C., 29, 32–3
Luxembourg Red Cross, 35,
146; Juniors, 104, 183

Mackinnon, Eleanor, 56, 57, 170
Magen Adom David, 25
Manga Arabs, 131–3
Memory of Solferino, A, 17–18,

21, 29, 44, 48, 153, 186
Mexican Red Cross, 144
Moroccan Red Crescent, 126, 165
Moynier, Gustave, 18, 19, 20, 21 34, 36, 46, 88

Nansen, Fridtjof, 114, 115, 116
Napoleon III, 11, 12, 28, 37
National Societies, 17–18, 18 19, 20, 21, 21–5, 29, 44, 45, 47, 48–50, 54, 55–6, 58, 87, 88, 89, 91, 100, 103, 105, 109, 110, 114–15, 116, 117, 119–20, 121, 123, 124, 125, 126, 127, 134–5, 138, 139, 141, 142, 144, 146–7, 148, 149, 151, 153, 154–5, 155–6, 157–8, 163, 165, 167, 169, 184, 186, 187
Netherlands Red Cross, 60, 65, 97, 136–8, 141, 146, 156, 161; Juniors, 179, 182
New Zealand Juniors, 175
Nightingale, Florence, 29, 43, 113, 149
Norwegian Red Cross, 60, 109, 139–140, 142

Oliver, Percy Lane, 59, 151

Pakistan Red Cross, 147
Paralysis Victims in Morocco, 156, 164–7
Persian Earthquake, 157–8
Philippines Red Cross, 164;
Polish Red Cross, 87, 109
Post-war Relief for Civilians, 55–6, 97, 99–100, 100–1, 102, 109, 110–13, 116, 124
Prisoners of War, 15, 35, 36, 41–2, 43, 47, 55, 67, 68, 72, 73, 74, 75, 76, 78, 79, 80, 81–2, 82–3, 94–5, 135

Red Lion & Sun Society of Iran (Persia), 24, 161
Refugees, 56, 66, 87, 97, 100,

101, 104, 105, 109, 114, 115; African Continent, 127, 172; German, 100, Jordan, 105; Korean, 109; Laotian, 126; Lebanon & Syria, 105; Spanish, 66; Vietnamese, 125, 126
Romanian Red Cross, 109, 146
Rombaut, Jeanne, 184–5
Russian Red Cross, 23, 48, 50

Service Hospitals Welfare, 86, 87, 109
Skopje, 158
Solferino, Battle of, 12, 13, 16, 17, 42, 186, 187, 188
South African Red Cross, 46, 82, 139, 145, 158
Spanish Red Cross, 67, 144
Swedish Red Cross, 48, 49, 60, 63–4, 110, 158, 161; Juniors, 184,
Swiss Red Cross, 35, 48, 49, 140, 161; Juniors, 179

Thai Red Cross (Siam), 140
Tibetan Refugees in Napal, 127–131
Tracing Service, 91, 92
Tristan da Cunha Islanders, 158–60; Juniors, 160
Tunisian Red Crescent, 23, 126;
Turkish Red Crescent, 23, 163;

Uruguayan Red Cross, 50

V.A.D.s, 50, 51, 52, 53, 54, 55, 59, 85, 86, 109

'White Ladies', 22, 94–5
Wounded and Sick, 13, 14, 15, 16, 17, 21, 26, 27, 30, 31, 32, 34, 35, 36, 39, 42, 45, 46, 47, 48, 49, 50, 52, 53, 54, 60, 85, 86, 87, 109

Yugoslav Red Cross, 116, 120–1; Juniors, 104